I HAVE BEEN BLESSED

I0539649

Cheryl Costello

Copyright © 2025 by Cheryl Costello

All rights reserved. No part of this book may be reproduced, distributed, or transmitted in any form or by any means, including photocopying, recording, or other electronic or mechanical methods, without the prior written permission of the publisher.

ISBN: 979-8-89397-436-2

Edition: First

Published by Reilly & Britton

DEDICATION

There are a few special people I would like to thank for making it possible for me to write this book. First, I must thank my husband Bill, for giving his life to me, for sharing every moment of our ups and downs, and for giving me the most wonderful blessings one could ever ask for. I would like to thank him for being my pillar of strength and thank him for holding me up when my life around me had crumbled down. Bill, I thank you with all my heart and soul.

I most definitely must thank my beloved son, Billy, for giving me twenty-six of the most extreme years of my life and all of his. Without Billy, this book would have been very dull and boring. Billy, the excitement of you will live in us forever.

And to my dearest daughter, Sharon, who just seems to grow stronger every day for me, you have become everything I ever dreamed of. I wish you all the best in your new marriage and pray that you will too, be blessed as I was with God's perfect children.

And last but not least I must thank my wonderful sister-in-law, Dolores, for all her support and blessed kindness. It was she who helped me get through this book. I thank you for your support, guidance, spirituality, and especially your typing. You too were my rock of Gibraltar. And a big thank you to Donna Cavanagh, for putting this all together.

TABLE OF CONTENTS

PROLOGUE

In the beginning, I was writing this book because I felt in many ways my story would touch many people. Being the not-so-traditional mom I had expected to be, and living the not-so-traditional life I expected to live, I somehow felt fulfilled putting it into words.

As time went on, I found out that life can throw you even more curves than you could ever expect. "God's Little Blessings" is a true story by a very weak but very strong woman. She shows there is no limit to a mother's love for her children. There is a series of events, one more profound than the other, and by her strength and the will of God, somehow the family seems to survive and overcome the flaws of life.

Because of some very unfortunate events, I was again encouraged to finish writing this book. The loss of my son would become my strength to continue.

A friend asked me what it was I wanted to accomplish by writing this book. First, I said I wanted to have it published, but most of all I wanted people to see my son Billy for what he really was. He was the glow in our lives. The fire that kept us going. He was the meaning of life, and he lived every single day of his life to the fullest. I would like parents to read this and realize there is more to life than just complaining about the little stuff and always being angry. I would like all the young adults to read this and know there is more to life than just today.

Life isn't always fair; we just have to pray for the will and the strength to go on.

THE BEGINNING

Let me tell you a little about myself. I was raised in a typical American household—you know, a mother, a stepfather, two sisters, and a stepbrother, whose ground we had to worship. From the time I was about ten or eleven years old, I wanted to grow up, get married, and be a mommy. I did not want to go to college or pursue any type of career. I was fascinated, or should I say brainwashed, by "Donna Reed" and "Father Knows Best." I was sure I could be the perfect wife and mother. I was an average child and wasn't much trouble to my mom. I set my goals all through school and achieved them.

One of my goals was to get out of my house. My stepfather was a groping snake. From the time I was ten years old until I left home to get married, I spent my life dodging him. I succeeded physically, but the mental scars will always be there. I never told my mother a thing until many years later for fear that she wouldn't believe me. And, as it was, she didn't believe me when I told her.

I married right out of high school at the age of eighteen. I fell head over heels for this Romeo, who was eighteen years older than I was. He was extremely good to me, except for one problem—he was an alcoholic. I did not know this at the time, because he only drank periodically, so no one figured the alcohol was what caused his mood swings.

I became pregnant right away. How exciting to have this wonderful life, God's blessing, inside your body, I thought. I was very healthy during the pregnancy, putting on more than forty pounds. I was ten days late when finally the labor started. On the way to the hospital, we had to stop and buy film–taking pictures is the most important of things. The delivery was perfect, with no complications at all. We now had an eight-pound, thirteen-ounce baby boy, named after my husband Bill, of course. We would call him Billy. Billy was Bill's pride and joy. We couldn't get enough pictures, especially since the film that was taken in the hospital was destroyed in a plane crash when sent out for developing.

It was about six weeks after the baby was born when God began to test us. I was over at a friend's house with Lil' Billy, who was so cute in his little outfit. Everyone was making a fuss over him. We were waiting for our husbands to come home for dinner when we got a phone call. My husband was test-driving a motorcycle and had an accident. I had to leave my baby there and drive to the hospital. His head was stitched up, he had a hole in his foot, and both arms and legs were in bad shape. He refused to stay in the hospital, so I took him home. Later, my son was brought home. I sat up for four days and nights watching both my babies in bed. This would only be the beginning of many hardships.

When Lil' Billy was four months old, I had a very serious car accident.

A man ran the red light and hit me broadside. At the time I felt fine. My mother-in-law was holding my son. They were both okay. Three days later I started having very bad headaches, along with memory loss and blacking out.

It took more than four months for the doctors to determine what exactly was wrong with me. During that time, I continued to be the best mom I could without getting help from anyone. My little son was no angel...he was now eight months old and had yet to sleep one night through. Then my doctor informed us that I needed a cerebral shunt, some type of tube to drain the fluid off my brain. This fluid was seven times the amount it was supposed to be and was causing a great deal of pressure on my brain. I didn't think the operation was a big deal. Heck, I was twenty years old and thought I was invincible.

After the surgery, I spent fourteen days upside down in bed so that my brain would come back naturally. After one more week, I left the hospital. Of course, I was completely bald. One good thing was that my mom came and trained Lil' Billy to sleep for me.

The headaches never went away but I learned to live with them. I continued to do all the things mommies are supposed to do, like the Easter bunny, birthday parties, Halloween, and Christmas.

This was about the time I got pregnant with blessing number two. I started to feel better; my headaches had eased up. I was having a lot of fun with my son. We built our first snowman and had a great Christmas. I just knew I was going to have a girl. That would just make everything perfect.

I was about seven months pregnant when my son became ill. First, he started with high fevers, which led to convulsions. Twice before First Aid arrived, he had stopped breathing. My husband had given him mouth-to-mouth and was able to revive him, but Bill was a complete basket case, and they would not let him ride in the ambulance, so he followed in the car. I sat with my son. He stopped breathing three more times. All I could do was pray out loud, hoping God would hear me. It hurt inside so bad to see that part of me lie lifelessly without a sound. Then just as we pulled into the hospital parking lot, he let out the most glorious scream. I knew my prayer was answered. My poor little boy had to go through so many tests, including a spinal tap. Oh, how we all cried. My husband and I took turns at the hospital. Bill had the nights, and I had the days. After about eight days, our little boy was able to come home.

The next three months were very quiet as we patiently awaited the arrival of blessing number two. Again, I was ten days late and so anxious I couldn't wait any longer. So, without my husband knowing, I drank castor oil. About six hours later, we were in the delivery room. This time I couldn't have an epidural because of my head injury, so I went all natural. No matter what other women say about the pain of bearing a child, you do remember it, even after seeing the baby. When the doctor said it was a girl, I said thank God, call it "quits." The doctor joked and said it was a funny name. Again, I had another perfect baby. Her head was round and full of black hair. We decided to call her Sharon. Sharon left the hospital in a little yellow dress, and barrettes in her hair. She was a perfect baby. At three days old, she slept eight hours through the night.

I thanked God for such a good baby because I was starting to not feel well again. The headaches were getting worse. I was able to organize and have her christening at the house, but only four weeks after her birth, I was back in the hospital. The shunt in my head had malfunctioned. The doctors guessed that it happened during the child's birthing. This time I was scared. I kept asking God, "Why me?" I just could not accept it, not again. I returned home after two weeks, bald. It was a little more difficult with two babies, but we managed. All three of us took a lot of naps.

It was only a month later when I started going into coma-like sleeps. It was very difficult to take steps without my head pounding. My sister-in-law and her husband took me back to the hospital, where I was told that the arteries where my tube went had collapsed. I needed surgery for the third time. I did not question God this time. I was sure that I was going to get through this because I had to take care of my babies.

It was a struggle with the pain and headaches, but as the months passed, I became stronger. Bill's drinking increased. And so did the physical abuse.

When my daughter was seven months old, I had my tubes tied. With all the problems I had after Sharon was born, in addition to my husband's physical abuse, I did not want to have any more children. My heart ached so badly, having done that to my body. And I felt so guilty betraying God like that. I only hoped that he would understand. Again, I was becoming a super-mom. Holidays and birthdays were celebrated with great enthusiasm. I taught the children how to swim. My son was two years old and my daughter was three months old. As she got older she had to do everything her brother did.

Lil' Billy started day care at three. Every day when I would drop him off, Sharon would throw a fit because she wanted to stay. The day care said that once she was potty trained, she would be able to attend. At sixteen months old, she was the youngest ever to start day care there. She and her brother were inseparable. They would run naked in our fenced-in yard, picking and eating mulberries. You couldn't ask for something more natural. I don't think I thanked God enough for those days.

One day, in the middle of the summer, Billy brings Sharon only about a year and a half old in from outside. He told me she had eaten the bad berries... ink berries, which are poisonous. I got in touch with the hospital's poison control center. They instructed me to get Ipecac syrup in her and follow her around with a little pail. Well, it did the trick. I had about half of a gallon of purple throw-up. Their dad was at the racetrack at the time, so he missed all the excitement.

I was about in my fourth year of marriage by this time. The kids were healthy and growing fast. My husband was drinking a little more often, which meant he was gone during the day, usually at the racetrack, and then he would go to the local bar at night. I didn't mind when he was away. I was always able to handle the children and keep the house clean. I began teaching my son to read. It was a lot of fun. Sharon could almost read at age two. I made my whole life evolve around my children. The less my husband was around, the better it was. He became violent at times, so I always had to walk on eggshells.

I started keeping two suitcases always packed. Every six months I would change from summer to winter clothes, and as for the children's clothes, I would go up a size. I always had to be prepared to leave if I had to. The only thing was that if I ever did leave, with or without the children I knew he would kill me. I would never leave my children. I would have to die for them first.

People married to alcoholics tend to do insane things. Maybe I should try drinking, I thought. Maybe I would fit in better. But after thinking about that one for a while, it didn't sound so good. Then I got really desperate one night and I prayed to the devil because I felt God was not listening to me. I then had the scariest dream I had ever had. It was so real that when I woke up, I cried and told God how sorry I was. I saw myself dead. They had dredged my car out of the creek and when they pulled me out, I was green. I could see my family crying, but they could not hear me telling them I was okay. I know that God had given me a sign that he truly was listening to me.

Death overwhelmed me. Deep in my heart, I believed I was going to die, and Bill was going to kill me. I wrote a poem and made a copy of it. I gave the copy to my sister and asked her to read it at my funeral. The poem was:

The time has come and we must part And say farewell to our dear hearts.

Should the darkness of the new found life Be brightened by the truthful light?

And pray that God will steer us straight And deliver us from this fearful hate.

We'll walk the grounds of trust and love

And feel the warmth from Him above.

I know now, that we're at peace

And locked-up feelings

Will release.

We have nothing to fear in this new way

We're here forever and ever to stay

I love you all, Cheryl

After a while of feeling sorry for myself, I got myself back into my so- called normal routine. Please don't get me wrong–I do love my husband, and I did then. When he was good, he was really good. He was a great father to the children. He always hugged and cuddled them. That was something I never had as a child, so it was a hard thing for me to learn to do. My life was like a roller coaster. Sometimes I loved him and sometimes I hated him. Most everybody saw the good side of Bill. Many would never believe me if I told them about a fight. I did not choose to tell many people about our problems.

For example, I never told my father anything.

He was such a quiet and reformed type of man, really, special to me. He saw something good in everything.

When there was a birthday or a holiday celebrated at our house we would have to do it twice, once with my mom and once with my dad. My sisters would come to both. I was very close with both of them.

Another year passed. Lil' Billy started kindergarten. I cried when he got on the bus and I waited the whole time on the front porch until he returned home. When he got off the bus, he was a different little boy. He wasn't mommy's little boy anymore. Then I sat down and began to cry again. He was angry because we never told him his name was William. When the teacher did roll call and said William Costello, Billy looked around the room to see who else had his last name.

It was about that same time Sharon started to take dancing lessons. She was so petite and cute. She had lost her front teeth at three years old when her brother accidentally drove a toy truck into her face. She also had stitches in her cheek, her chin, and her mouth. She was a tough cookie. You could hardly see any of her scars as she grew older. When she was four years old, the dentist made her a plate with two little false teeth. She wouldn't leave the house without having her teeth in her mouth.

Since both of their birthdays are only a month apart, I would give them one big birthday party. There would be anywhere from twenty to thirty children in my backyard. They would have clowns, magicians, and even pony rides.

I had this need, or maybe you would call it a guilt feeling, about having my tubes tied. I felt God was angry with me. I had suggested to my husband about adopting. One of the problems was that he had a very long arrest record. Even though it was many years ago, it would still put a damper on any chance of adopting. This want for another child smoldered inside of me. Around this same time, my husband had surgery on his back. He was in an auto accident and had to have a disc removed. I visited him regularly and at the same time, I was not feeling well. He came home from the hospital in March during a snowstorm. I was outside shoveling when I started to get terrible pains in my abdomen. After the second attack, I called my gynecologist. I explained to him that I had been bleeding for fourteen days and that the pain felt like labor. He started screaming at me. "I tied your tubes four years ago. This is all in your head. You don't need a gynecologist. You need a doctor for your head." He told me to take two aspirins and sleep on a heating pad.

So, I did this for a week until I was rushed to the hospital. I had emergency surgery for a ruptured tubal pregnancy. I had walked around a whole week in pain with that poison spreading through my body, all because that doctor did not want to admit he did not tie my tubes correctly. I had seen him twice in the eight weeks prior to that because I wasn't feeling right. I switched doctors after that. So once again, I was in the hospital for major surgery. This time it was my birthday. As always, my husband was by my side when I needed him. I do believe, because I had thought so strongly about it, I believe that is what caused the pregnancy.

THE LAST BIG FIGHT

This brings us to the summer of our seventh year. Lil' Billy was six years old, and Sharon was four. Billy was very protective of his little sister. Whenever his father got loud, Billy took Sharon into his room. Well, it was August eighteenth. We were celebrating both of my sisters' birthdays since they are a day apart. My mom and uncle were over, they too were big drinkers, so my husband sat around all day drinking with them. He was telling them stories about when he was in jail. I used to get upset when he talked about any of that in front of the children. I didn't want them to know that part of his life, at least not at an early age. The party was over and everyone left except my mom. She came up from Florida and stayed with us.

I walked into the bedroom where Bill was lying down. I remember saying something like "I love you, but sometimes I can't stand you." I was referring to him always boasting about being in jail or how he wound up in jail. At that point, his face became twisted and he began to bite down on his lower lip. I knew then that, that was something I shouldn't have said. He stood up on the bed and in a deep raging voice he shouted, "Sometimes I hate you." Then he began swinging with a closed fist. After the first two punches, I was numb. I ran into Sharon's room to get away but also to warn my mother and the children to stay away. He followed me in punching doors as he entered Sharon's room. He grabbed the two-foot bed post from the foot of my daughter's bed. First, he hit me in the stomach. It was more like a jab. I then ran back into my bedroom pleading with him to stop. The children were screaming. I did not hear or see my mother. I was hit once again by the bed post. This time to the right side of my head. I was knocked unconscious. When I came to for a minute, I heard Lil' Billy telling his father not to kill mommy. Then I came again and I heard my husband on the phone. Something must have snapped in his head. He had called the police. I left in the ambulance, and he left with the police.

After two days in the hospital with a fractured skull and a concussion, I went to my girlfriend's house where my children were. I remained there for about two weeks. At that point in my life, I was completely lost. I would walk in circles in the house just crying. I didn't know where to go or what to do. Then I came upon a picture of Jesus on the wall. I just opened my heart and let Him in. I begged Him to straighten out my life because I was unable to. I needed all the guidance I could get.

I did not intend to go back home. I had to do what was best for my children. My mom and sisters threatened me that if I went back, they would never speak to me again. They would consider me dead. Two weeks passed and I had to meet with Bill in court to agree on some type of visitation privileges. Bill had spoken with my dad. My dad told my husband that maybe this happened for the best. Bill could not understand why my father would say such a thing after his daughter was just beaten.

Bill informed me that he was entering rehab. The children and I were now staying at another girlfriend's house. Another two weeks had passed and I went and spoke with a counselor. It was then she told me that my husband was an alcoholic. I said, "Thank God. I thought he was a skitzo." Every time I tried to talk to someone for help, they wouldn't believe my husband could be that mean. They had never seen that side of him. This was such a relief to hear that he was an alcoholic and there was a good chance to control his actions.

I tried to do my best to explain to the children their daddy's problem. They seem to understand it well. Sharon, who was only four at the time, was playing outside with another child when she was asked why her dad was in the hospital. She quickly came back with, "My dad gets mean when he drinks too much beer." My son Billy was much more emotional. Although I thought he was very strong, he was hiding everything. He wrote his father a letter that brought tears to my eyes.

This was his letter:

Dear Dad,

I cry when I love you Feels like you come out in every tear.

I don't want you to ever die because I really love you.

I really miss you, Daddy. Want to see you again. I love you very much.

Love, Billy

Six weeks had passed when I finally moved back home with the children.

I decided that this family was worth saving, no matter what other people felt I should do. This was what my dad meant when he said this happened for the better. My mom and sisters stopped communicating with me. This is my life and I'm going to make it work, I thought. We anxiously awaited Bill's discharge.

The children were so excited to be home. They ran through the rooms as if it were a brand-new house. It felt good to play with the animals and sweep my own floors. The anticipation of his arrival was somewhat nerve-racking. I was excited but extremely nervous. I helped the children make a welcome home sign. It had two Cabbage Patch Kids on it with the words - "Welcome Home." We hung it in the hallway, so he would see it as soon as he walked in the front door.

I drove to the hospital and parked in the front circle. His bags were waiting on the top of the steps. He loaded them into the car and got in the driver's seat. There we sat alone for the first time in about six weeks. He kissed me, a kiss that was like a first kiss. I thought to myself, "Oh my God, I really do love him." We actually parked the car on the back of the property and made love before we went to the house.

My husband came home and life was unbelievable. We were on what some call a "pink cloud." I fell in love all over again. The children were so relaxed. This was what I always thought life should be—just like "Donna Reed" and "Father Knows Best."

MOVING ON...GROWING

STRONGER

Billy was now in first grade and doing very well. He seemed to be well-adjusted to the whole situation. Sharon was in day care. She was smart as a whip. It was when I had her tested by the child study team at the age of three and a half that I found out just how smart she was. They said she had the mentality of a seven-year-old, and they also felt she should already be in school. The Board of Education refused her, saying she was too young. I was the class mom and very busy with school. I was also making cupcakes and organizing the parties for each holiday. I enjoyed every minute of being with the children.

Another year passed and I began having an urge to have another baby.

Our lives were perfect now. I wanted another baby so bad that I became obsessed with it. I discussed this with my new gynecologist. He recommended a doctor at the University for me to see. After a few tests and minor surgery, I was told that my one tube could be reversed, so I went through a very painful and expensive surgery. The whole thing cost us about twenty-six thousand dollars. Call me insane, but I thought this was my only way of getting on graven simulacrum's side. I felt he would now forgive me and bless me with another healthy child.

I was now on my way to trying to have another child. The children were very excited. My son told his teacher I was getting untied—with children there are no secrets. I remained very busy with the school, involved in everything. The children would win every Halloween contest for the best costume.

First Lil' Billy was in soccer. He was very active and his grades were exceptional. Then, of course, Sharon had to join his soccer team, and what a brute she was. They were so cute in their bright-colored T-shirts and their little white shorts. Billy never showed any remorse for his father's drinking from years before. He seemed very stable and healthy. Sharon didn't remember much of anything, which was great. We seemed to be a very normal family. My husband continued his program. Sometimes we would go as a family to his meetings. One time before the meeting started, my son, who was now eight years old, grabbed the mike and said, "My name is Billy and I'm not an alcoholic." We were glad that he was open about his father's problem.

A couple of years passed. They seemed to go so quickly. I guess it's when you have problems that the time just seems to drag on. My husband was now starting a new habit one that I really didn't approve of. This was the racehorse business. I loved the horses, but what I didn't like was the gambling part. I grew up in a household that evolved around the horse business. My stepfather would train the horses, and my mother would bet on them. If the horses didn't win, we didn't eat. I certainly didn't want those kinds of worries again. Needless to say, I had to let my husband have this one vice. This was much better than his drinking.

The children remained very active in sports and other activities. All Lil' Billy talked about was football, even in his sleep. Sharon had me busy with dance on Monday, organ lessons on Tuesday, and CCD on Wednesday, which they both went to. Then she had soccer on Thursday in the afternoon and acting in the evening, and at last, there was gymnastics on Friday. They both had games on Saturday. My daughter would complain that she had a free day on Sunday and wanted to sign up for some other type of activity. I'm just glad I had them when I was young because I know there is no way I could spread myself that thin now. In between all this, my husband and I would find time to try and make another baby.

Whatever Sharon puts her mind to, she succeeds. One Christmas when she was seven years old, we were with the Brownies at a Christmas Tree Lighting Ceremony when Little Miss New Jersey lit the tree. That's what she wanted to be, she told me. It was about six months later when I entered her in The Young Miss New Jersey Pageant. I made her a beautiful pink satin gown. All four of us went to the hotel for the pageant. To our surprise, there are few professionals there. When it came to modeling Sharon had no experience whatsoever. Bill began to yell at me. "How could you enter in something like this? She'll never win this competition."

The last part of the pageant was the most important. All they judged on was your beauty. One of the teenagers helped her by showing her how to walk in a gown. I sat my daughter down and told her not to worry. "If all they were judging on was beauty, heck, you have to win because nobody is as pretty as you." Well, when they announced her name as the next New Jersey Natural Young Miss, we were all ecstatic. Bill must have jumped a foot out of his seat. That was the beginning of our little beauty queen's future.

Things began to change with my son Billy. It seemed the harder he tried to fit in with his friends, the more they wouldn't let him. Mostly all the boys who played football lived in the developments and came from the city. My children only knew what the country was like because we lived on a small farm. He was intimidated by them, which finally led him to quit football. He also quit playing soccer after that. He had a problem with authority figures and seemed to be changing before our eyes. It used to break my heart when his so- called best friends had pool parties and did not invite him. All he wanted was to just belong.

Well, a year and a half had passed and I still wasn't pregnant. The doctor sent me to the hospital for another test. They shot dye into me to see if the tube was blocked. With just a little bit of pain the test was finished, and on the TV screen was my tube with the dye flowing through it. They said there was no problem, just go home and keep trying. So we did. Four months later I became pregnant, but before we could get excited, I miscarried. At least we knew we could do it.

We all just continued with our lives, Sharon was in a couple more competitions. She won a few more small titles. Every other month she was in the newspaper. She was very popular with the boys and not so popular with the girls. Her brother always had to hear something about his sister being in the paper. I am sure he resented her for it, and for us giving her the attention.

Even though we were always there for him and his sports, it just wasn't the same. We didn't think it bothered him at the time, even though a few people had asked us if he was jealous of his sister.

We bought a racehorse and named her "I Am Trouble." This was my husband's newest pride and joy. We raised her in the yard. When she was three there was a big series at Meadowlands Racetrack. She took first, two seconds, and a third. She made a lot of money and we had many pictures taken with her. The children didn't like the horses. I guess they were jealous at the time we gave to them. We would go to the farm on weekends and to the races on the nights that she raced. They were so used to me giving every minute to them that it was hard for them to understand that I needed to spend some time with their father. This doesn't mean I wasn't still active with my children, or I should say with my daughter. Billy started drawing away from us. He was keeping much more to himself and his new friends, who were certainly different from the others. They didn't care about school, sports, family, or even themselves for that matter. All they did was hang out. My son's whole attitude began to change. He started doing poorly in school and I began receiving phone calls from the vice principal.

Sharon was still very active in the pageant department. When she was ten years old, she won the New Jersey Miss National Pre-Teen Pageant, an even bigger thrill than the other title. She got a full-page article in the press and appeared at the mall and in parades. She started modeling in New York. She was the size ten model for a large clothing company. She did print work for schoolbooks and sales magazines. I now had my own little professional.

Mentally she was two years ahead of the girls in her class which sometimes made it very hard to deal with her.

THE NATIONALS

We had to now prepare for the Nationals. We had less than three months to get it all together. Since my daughter was now "Famous," she felt she should have some of the things the famous people had, like a miniature Vietnamese pot-belly pig. So, one night about nine o'clock, this hillbilly type man comes knocking at my door. In his southern accent, he told me he had my pig. My husband forgot to inform me of this. So yes, we now had a pig living in our house. Her name was Bacon. She only remained in the house for about a month. Those types of pigs have to be starved to remain small. Bacon now lives in the garage and weighs about two hundred pounds. I am the only one who gives her any attention—another disowned pet.

Anyway, the nationals in Florida were going to be through the week of Thanksgiving. I made sure all my Christmas shopping was finished because I knew there would be much confusion when we came back from Florida. I would still have to do the Christmas Bazaar at the school. Meanwhile, I had missed my period. Yes, I was pregnant. I took the at-home test, and the little ball turned green. I told my husband but asked him not to tell anyone until we made sure everything was okay. Not even the children knew.

I told my son to bring a friend with him. I felt this would help in not making him feel so left out with all the attention on Sharon. So, the day came and we all piled into the van to drive down to Florida. There was my daughter, my son, his friend, my brother, his new wife, my husband driving, and me. We had a large conversion van. Sharon had about twelve pieces of luggage all to herself. We go to the hotel one day early. My husband stayed one night and then flew back home to take care of the animals. This way we had a vehicle to use there for the week.

The practices began very early the next day, so I was on the go with my daughter from morning till night. Billy and his friend were able to come and go as they pleased. My brother and his wife left to visit friends for a few days.

We had tickets to Universal Studios. The boys could have had the run of the place, but they both caught the flu. Both of them sat on a curb outside the Hard Rock Café, sick as dogs. The day was really cold too. The next day would be Thanksgiving. This would be the first one I was celebrating without my husband. I really felt different.

I wasn't feeling well that night. I started to get really slow. Then I began to bleed—another miscarriage. I wasn't able to cry because I couldn't let the kids know what was happening. I couldn't upset my daughter. This was her special week. I was pretty sick the next day. I had a lot of cramps and it was very hard to walk around. I remember my daughter saying, "Hurry up.

You're walking like an old lady." I also began to get this twitch on the left side of my face, which was very painful, not to mention, funny-looking. My mind just would not concentrate and I couldn't think straight. Anyway, I made it to the airport to pick up my husband. He was coming in for the big event. We were waiting for him in the lobby. Sharon had on a fuchsia silk shirt with a tiny black pleated skirt. She also had fuchsia tights and a fuchsia hat on. She looked like a little French girl. I enjoyed watching her while we waited for her dad to arrive.

Finally, he arrived. He walked right up to me and before he kissed me, he said, "What the hell happened to you?" He was referring to my face. I couldn't believe it was that noticeable. I guess I was in really bad shape. I had all the symptoms of a nervous breakdown, but I told him not to worry. I just had to get through this pageant and get home.

The pageant came and went. Sharon only won a scrapbook award.

We were all greatly disappointed, but we knew we would survive. Again, we piled into the van and began our venture home. Also, my son had talked his father into buying a two-foot iguana, so it too was in the van with us. He was to become known as Fred. All the way home the only thing I could think about was losing another baby. I did all I could not to cry. It was a good thing we didn't tell anybody and get them excited for nothing. No one talked much so it seemed like an eternity. Finally, we reached home. The twitches in my head had stopped and I became more relaxed.

I made an appointment with my G.Y.N. on December tenth just to make sure everything was okay with me. The blood tests came back and everything was good and negative to the pregnancy. Once again, I became a super mom. I did the Christmas bazaar at the children's school. I did all the ordering, selling, and returning the leftovers to the company. I always helped the school make a pretty good profit.

MY LAST CHANCE

On December seventeenth I started my special novena to Baby Jesus. You see between the seventeenth and the twenty-fifth of December is the most powerful time, since it is the Feast of the Nativity of Christ the Infant. I was praying to Baby Jesus to help me conceive again. I was due on the twenty-fifth to get my period. I did not get it. I knew my prayers were answered. I was feeling pretty good and just a little bit queasy. This time I did not say anything to anybody, not even my husband. On January tenth, I had an argument with my son in the backyard. I don't really recall what it was about, all I remember was turning fast to go to the steps and falling. After that, I had a slight pain in my lower stomach. This was when I decided to tell Bill that I was pregnant.

The next day I went to the hospital for a pregnancy test and an HCG level, which shows the blood levels that increase as the baby grows. I had my first set of tests on the thirteenth. The doctor called me that night and congratulated me.

He also said that I should go on Thursday morning, the sixteenth, and have another HCG test taken.

It was around two in the afternoon when the doctor's office called.

First, he said the HCG count went up, but he didn't feel it was enough. His nurse then got on the phone and gave me instructions to drink thirty-two ounces of water and go to the out-patient unit at the hospital. I went into a room where a female technician began a test. While she was moving the instrument over my stomach, trying to see something, she said that they could pick up the fetus as early as seven weeks. I told her that I was only at the most five weeks pregnant.

I was then instructed to empty my bladder since the other test did not require any water. Easier said than done—do you know how hard it is to try and get thirty-two ounces of water out of your body after holding it for such a long time? Well, I tried my best, which wasn't good enough. They kept sending me back to the bathroom but I just was not able to get rid of all the water.

This next test was a probe instrument. This time there was also a male technician in the room. Then the nurse said that my doctor was there. I looked up and said that he wasn't my doctor— I had never seen him before in my life. He introduced himself and said he was from the same medical group.

While looking at the screen, they all commented on how much water was in my bladder. They were not able to see anything else. Then this doctor said he saw a bulge in my left tube and began asking me all kinds of questions, such as what type of surgery I had and how was I with anesthesia. I asked him why and he then said that he felt I had another tubal pregnancy. Then I told him I didn't feel like this with the last one. I didn't have any pain or bleeding. He then said that my left tube looked disfigured, and I explained it was reconstructed. I thought my doctor should have given this guy a little bit of background before sending him to take his place. I mean, he wasn't even thinking when he gave me the instructions to drink all that water when he knew I could only be five weeks pregnant. He was the one who took the pregnancy test on December tenth, which was negative.

The doctor had my husband and I was scared and confused. He said he thought he saw blood by the tube, which meant it was ready to rupture. He told my husband it was better to have me alive than to risk not having the surgery, and that he would be doing the surgery with a scope, so there would be hardly any scar and a quick recovery. My doctor came in that night to reassure me that his associate was very good and tried to calm me down. He boasted that he was the best in the office with the scope. I made it known that only if it was absolutely necessary were they to touch my tube. I knew this was my last chance to get pregnant.

The next morning came and I was prepped for surgery. The doctor walked into my room and told me he decided to do a C-section instead of the scope. I did not understand then. This type of surgery is a couple of thousand dollars more, and the stay in the hospital is three days longer. The anesthesiologist was also confused. He kept asking me why I was having this operation. In his opinion, he felt I should wait it out. My state of mind at the time was nearly over the edge.

The operation was over. I was lying in the very cold recovery room. I don't know if it was actually cold in there or if I was just in shock after the anesthesia. I could hear people talking, but I was kind of out of consciousness. I recognized one of the people speaking. It was my anesthesiologist. I heard him gloating to the nurse, saying, "So there wasn't any atopic pregnancy after all." I tried to look around the room to see if there were any other patients in there with me. There were none. I asked the nurse what the doctor had done. She said he would be up to my room later to talk to me.

Later, in my room, I told Bill what I thought I heard. He was speechless. Then my doctor came in. He explained that the pregnancy was on the outside of the tube, and he had to remove the tube. Since the operation, I had begun to bleed a great deal. The anesthesiologist paid me one last visit. I did not say what I heard in the recovery room. He asked if my doctor had told me what he did. I said he had told me the pregnancy was on the outside of the tube and he removed it. He said, "That's right, he removed your tube." He also told me that if I had any more surgery I should be careful because while I was under my heart had skipped a few beats. Then he left. I spent two more days in the hospital not remembering much. I was suffering from total depression.

A friend from the church came to console me. She laid her hands on me and prayed. I really felt God had done this to me and this was my punishment from years back. She assured me that God had nothing to do with this. It was all in the doctor's hands. I actually did not understand what she meant then, but I would soon find out.

Five days had passed since I had gone under the knife. I had a seven-inch incision with eleven staples in it which had to be removed. I went into the doctor's office and slowly lay down on the table. While the doctor was removing the staples, he went over his findings. First, he said the growth on the outside of the tube had no pregnancy in it either. So, I did hear correctly in the recovery room, I thought. My head began to boil. First, I told him I had already known that and asked him why it took him five days to tell me. I began to throw all kinds of questions at him, or should I say statements because I was not waiting for any answers. I told him there was probably too much water and asked where the pregnancy was. I said we could have waited a couple of days and if I was miscarrying it would have happened naturally. This explained all the bleeding after the operation. I was miscarrying then. You see, they took blood every day after the operation. I was still pregnant, but now the HCG level was going down.

So, I left the hospital after all that surgery and I was still pregnant, but miscarrying now because of the surgery. I knew this was not an act of God but an act of stupidity on behalf of a money-hungry medical group. I tried to sue the bastards, but it was nearly impossible. They had a way to get around everything. In fact, I was turned over to a collection agency for the balance after my insurance paid them. To this day, six years later, I still make payments of ten dollars a month.

OH GOD, TAKE THE WANT AWAY

I was pretty low at this point in my life. I somehow had to face the fact that I was not going to have any more children and I had better make good with what I had. It was difficult to go anywhere, I didn't want to see anybody pregnant or with a new baby. I felt so cheated. I had even written my original doctor a letter, a sarcastic thank-you note. I thanked him for recommending his associate and I hoped his day off went a little bit better than the day I had in the hospital. I told him I was physically getting better, but mentally it was going to take a lot longer. I explained to him that I could not understand how his partner could lie so much on the medical report and live with himself. I really felt he did not have the right to play God. He had damaged me physically, mentally, and financially. I said that if I were him I would not have put such recommendations in his partner, nor would I pass my patient to the next guy like an old shoe.

I knew this depression had to end. I began to pray again, but this time I prayed that God would take the want away. And little by little, He did just that.

Our son was beginning to change right before our eyes. The church no longer had a place in his world, nor did his family. He was fifteen now and thought the world owed him. If he was grounded, he would sneak out at night. It's against the law to hit your child, and anyway, if my husband started to hit him I would stop him because I knew he would get carried away. Bill still had a temper and I didn't like to see it flare up.

One night Billy confided in me that he had all this hatred for his father for everything that he had done to me years back. He said he only started to remember things when he was about twelve years old. Well, that explained a lot to me. He told me if he could, he would kill him. He was crying so hard when he was telling me this that I knew deep down he really loved his father but had so many mixed feelings in his head. I tried to explain that, things were different and told him his father did not hit me anymore. But he said, "Every time he gets mad and starts to yell I think he's going to." The memories of that last fight were smoldering in his head. I knew my son was going to need some serious help. There was just no way I could tell my husband that his son, his flesh and blood, hated him so much that he wanted him dead.

Billy was a freshman and already a threat to the teachers. We transferred him to a private school. We thought it would help, but no such luck. He did well as far as grades went, but he was depressed not to be hanging out with his friends. So, after the marking period, we transferred him back to the public high school. No matter what type of deal we made with him, he never kept up his end of the bargain.

I was beginning to despise teenagers. I just kept telling myself little babies grow up to be nasty teenagers. This was helping me cope with my desire for children.

At this point, my daughter seemed to be no problem. She wanted to attend Catholic school, so for her seventh grade, she went to the local Catholic school affiliated with our church. Her grades were superb. Her attitude was pretty good although she kept pretty much to herself and had no special friends for that entire year. She was trying to prove some kind of point. The teachers and sisters didn't seem to care for her, I think because she had talked to boys. I guess they didn't understand that when you have a brother just two years older, you're going to know a lot of boys. There were a few times she would come home crying after getting yelled at because she stayed after to watch them play football in the church parking lot. I then would get on the phone and make a few threats of my own. She ended that year with straight A's and a few angry teachers hoping she wouldn't come back.

There was one flaw that my daughter had. She was a chronic complainer, a hypochondriac. But, after so many years you tend to know what is real and what isn't. Anyway, she had been over at the high school with a couple of her older friends when she came home hopping in the front door. She proceeded to lay on the floor holding her foot in the air, screaming "I think I broke it!" Every week she would come home with something. She thought it was broken, so I made her go to bed and I put ice on it.

Later that night I told my husband that if it was swollen or red in the morning, I would take her to the doctor, just in case. So, morning came, and off to the doctor we went. And, yes, she did fracture her fibula, or whatever. You can just imagine the ribbing I got for making her wait all night with a broken foot. My only response was that she had cried wolf one time too many.

As for my son, let's just say he passed freshman year. During the summer break, I began to get very sick. I could not bend my knees or my elbows. I could only move very slowly. It was almost like going backward. I lost all my short-term memory and would have to write down every little thing. I would go to the food store in town and get lost. I really thought I was losing my mind. Many days I would stay in bed; I think sometimes I forgot what I was supposed to do once I did get up. This went on for about two months when I finally went to the doctor. As a parent, you always think you can make yourself better. Now if it was my husband or one of my children, I would have had them to the doctor immediately. But anyway, I finally did go, and when all the blood tests came back, he said I was very lucky. I had Lymes disease, it was in the fourth stage. I really didn't know what that meant exactly, but it wasn't very good. Immediately I was put on IV antibiotics which I would have for several weeks. It wasn't bad though. I didn't have to go to the hospital. I was able to give myself the injections daily through a tube that was temporarily in my vein.

I don't remember dealing with the children much then. I don't remember dealing with much of anything for quite a while. The summer passed as if it never was. The new school year was starting all over again. I really wasn't looking forward to this. I still had the IV in but I was moving around much better. I was even able to think for myself sometimes. The other times I would write messages on my hands so I would remember. Good thing I didn't forget how to read. I know it sounds a little childish, but it worked. It became a way of life for me, still some to this day.

Sharon went back to Catholic school, this time to give them hell, I think. We paid all her tuition and bought all new uniforms. After about her third week there, she came home crying again. I said that was enough. I went to the school and transferred her out. I was told they could not refund any of my money. I said that was fine and that in my envelope every Sunday I would leave the Father a note saying I gave it at school. The Sister said she was sorry I felt that way. I really didn't write the Father that note, but I was pissed.

So back my daughter went to her old public school. I wasn't sure if it was a good move or not. But who was I to make any decisions at that point in my life, in my state of mind? Billy started the sophomore year with a bang.

IT'S ALL DOWNHILL

One night, at about two AM, there was a knock at the door, the first of many knocks in the middle of the night. It was the township police, they said they had reason to believe our son had a gun in his possession. I stood there numb, hoping this was all a mistake. My husband rushed into Billy's room and woke him. He told us that at one point he did have a gun here, but had since given it to a friend. He got fingerprinted and had his picture taken. He seemed to be falling into his father's footsteps without us even realizing it. After all the legal mumbo jumbo, Billy was placed on two-year's probation. Also, around the same time as the gun incident, I found out my son was doing some pretty heavy drugs. I mean all kinds of drugs...acid, coke, pot...just about anything he could get his hands on. So he now had to attend an out-patient rehab facility, which was a big joke.

My son was on a roll you might say. There would be a chain of events that would make your hair stand on edge, each one more unbelievable than the last. Many tried to tell me this was a stage. I really didn't think a stage would last as long as this would. Every week or two I would call another longtime girlfriend up and give her the run-down of the events for that week. Then I realized I was beginning to scare her. You see, her children were only toddlers at the time. She must have been

I Have Been Blessed

having nightmares of them growing up, so I stopped dumping on her.

Meanwhile, we were beginning to have some serious problems with my daughter. First of all, her modeling career was coming to a quick end. You see, she was still five feet tall and wasn't going to grow any taller. Her body wasn't that of a little girl, so she couldn't do children's clothing anymore. She seemed very disgusted with herself. She quit gymnastics and danced and bleached her beautiful brown hair white. I could not believe this was my daughter. A three-time beauty queen was now a white-haired, angry girl in huge, baggy clothes. She also began to smoke and drink. She hated her brother with passion. She knew all of what her brother was doing long before we found out, but she kept it all inside. It was eating at her at a fast rate. To top it all off, she was border line suicidal. I know a lot of it was for attention, and a lot was out of depression. Her brother would get violent with her when we weren't home. But then she would beg us not to say anything to him because he would be worse the next time.

Trying to deal with both of these children was certainly taking the want away. I was beginning to hate children, all children. The end of the school year came. Billy passed his sophomore year, by the skin of his teeth. It wasn't that he was stupid. He just didn't give a damn.

Sharon on the other hand had come around. She dyed her hair back to brown and began wearing some appealing clothing. Now I would say that was a stage she went through. Through her ordeal, her grades had never suffered. She was a straight 'A' student. In fact, she graduated eighth grade with the highest honors award. That was in all her subjects. Once again, we were very proud of her accomplishments. She kept her distance from her brother, almost as if they were in two different worlds.

GIVING HIM AWAY

It was October and the beginning of my son's junior year in high school. I was just hoping this year would be better than the last, or should I say the last two years. My daughter was just beginning her first year in high school, a brand-new freshman. The world was like an open book to her, and she was like a sponge to it. She was really willing to absorb everything she came in contact with. She was beautiful and already very popular. Many of the upper- class men knew her and had a lot of respect for her. She was everything I ever wished I could be. To have all that with an outgoing personality, who could ask for anything more?

There was one problem—her brother. Nobody, I mean no males, could even look at her, let alone talk to her. He regulated her outfits each day. The teachers never compared the two, or maybe they did and just took to liking Sharon. She immediately joined the student council and began to make an impression on the school.

Billy, on the other hand, was making an impression on his own. He became a real tough guy, especially with the women teachers. He was immediately suspended for threatening a teacher's life. He was big with words, but I'm sure he could never follow through with his threats. We were just about one month into the new school year and going nowhere. The teachers didn't want him in school and he was just sixteen. So what was he going to do out of school? He was still on probation for another year and things were looking pretty bad. We couldn't send him to military school because we didn't have the money. I talked to my nephew in Virginia Beach about the whole situation, and out of what I thought was the kindness of his heart, he offered to take care of Billy down there.

After thinking this out carefully, both my husband and I agreed that this might be the best thing for him. We looked at it from all angles. He would be starting fresh in a new school, leaving his bad reputation behind. He was very bright in school so he would have no problems with his grades. This seemed like the perfect solution.

It took about a week to make all our arrangements up here and we took off for Virginia Beach. The six-and-a-half-hour ride was very gloomy.

Sharon had taken a couple of days off from school to keep me company. Billy wasn't speaking much to me, and I understood why. I was taking him away from his life, his school, his friends. I had many mixed feelings about this whole thing. I kept telling myself that it was the best thing for everyone. I really believed that by taking my son out of the environment I would be helping him, maybe saving his life.

I cannot explain the sick feeling that took over my body. The tears would just fill up in my eyes, but I would not let them flow. Deep, deep down inside I felt like I was deserting my son, abandoning him, but I didn't know what else to do. Our lives were unmanageable at home. Something had to be done.

After three days of signing all sorts of legal papers, it was done. My son now belonged to my nephew. Still, he wasn't speaking to me, which didn't help my frame of mind. I just had to keep telling myself it was the right thing to do. He had his own room, new clothes, and a new school. He was going to live somewhat like a bachelor now, maybe have a few more responsibilities.

My daughter and I left. Now everything seemed gloomy. The truck was really empty but we tried to make the best of the ride home. My daughter told me about a boy she was interested in from school. She said that he was a senior and almost seventeen. That didn't sound too bad. He was about two and a half years older than her. But, like I said before, she was much more mature for her age. There was one more thing she asked me. Did it bother me that he was Spanish? I said no, as long as he respects you. The ride seemed to get a little better as we got closer to home.

The next day came and it was hell. I had this real bad feeling for days, maybe weeks. All I could do was cry. I had a lot of resentment towards my husband. I really did believe that a lot of this was Bill's fault, and he should have been able to do something about this. I wasn't sleeping at night and when I did, I would dream terrible nightmares about my son. I began to clean, which seemed to be the only way for me to get through the days.

I'm sure every woman dreams of that feeling of having everything accomplished—all the laundry finished, the floors washed and vacuumed, and everything dusted and polished, just so you could sit down and relax with your feet up. Well, that's a bunch of bull because through this ordeal I just kept cleaning until there wasn't anything left to clean and all I was left with was more time to sit and think about my son. After eight days I still couldn't go into his room, nor would I let anyone else in there. I kept telling myself he was just away at school as if he had gone off to college. But in my heart, I knew he was there because we put him there. I had to stop crying because I couldn't let anyone really see how I felt.

Thanksgiving came and we had a nice celebration with our small family, including my nephew and of course, Billy. This was the first time I had seen him since Halloween when I left him in Virginia. He looked great. He seemed to be adjusting well. He said he had met a few friends, including a girlfriend. He was always a Romeo. My son and my nephew seemed to be getting along really well. There was laughter and jokes at the table. We gave thanks to the Lord for this special occasion. The two days they stayed certainly weren't long enough. They had to leave to go back to Virginia, so once again the tears began to fall as I watched them pull out of the driveway. This time I was a little more relaxed, thinking that everything was fine.

I took a day for myself and went to visit a childhood girlfriend. I really needed a break from my house. I brought Sharon with me. It had been six years since I had even seen my girlfriend and her children. She was the same sweet girl I had known for most of my life. It felt good to talk and share with her. Our visit was only for a couple of hours, but it really did help me. When I came home that night, I felt compelled to write her a letter:

Dear Friend,

I remember the first time we met. You brought out a paper plate with slices of oranges. We sat in that circle behind the Coffee's house and ate them. We were just two little happy girls. I even remember how you lied to me, saying you were almost two years older than you were. Life was so fun and simple then. Everything seemed exciting and important, like the little plays we would put on for the neighborhood or the funerals we would have for all the dead birds we would find.

Remember how close we were? We never kept a secret from each other. We knew the neighborhood like a book. How about those carnivals we had and how we would take all the money we made and go straight to Jersey Freeze? Do you remember the first time you dropped your ice cream and how funny it sounded? Every time after you would drop it just to laugh.

How about us being blood sisters and spit sisters? There wasn't really anything that kept us apart. Except for that one fight where we didn't talk for about six months. And wasn't it funny how we both got Valentine's cards from each other (thanks to our moms)? Your mom was always great, especially for a hug. I get a little choked up thinking, or should I say missing, those old times. To tell the truth, I'm crying right now. I've become very emotional in my old age. Isn't that funny? One day you're a little girl and the next day you're grown -up with a whole lot of worries. It's really funny how the time has just passed by so fast. I tried to keep a spot in my mind and in my heart to always remember all our good and bad times together.

Yes, it was really great seeing you after six years. It was as if no time had come between us. It will always be that way. We now have kids of our own, and they too are going through some fun and difficult times. I pray that we can be there for them as we were for each other. Please keep this letter since it is the first letter I've written you in twenty-seven years. I don't know if I will ever write another one like this. I too, am making a copy to keep it fresh in my mind and close to my heart.

I know you are always there for me, and I hope you know I am here for you. Again it was really great seeing you, and remember our bodies may change, but the vision I have of you is from many years ago. This kind of sounds like a love letter. It's not meant to. I just really had this little voice in my head telling me to put it on paper before I forget.

Please keep in touch, Love, Cheryl.

Being able to look back on happy times sort of became a crutch for me. I don't know if it was an easy way out or even a healthy way out, but it was a way out, nonetheless.

MISSING IN VIRGINIA

It was on a Thursday night when I got a phone call. It was about ten PM and my nephew was on the other end. He asked if we had heard from Billy. He seemed to have been missing since that morning when he supposedly left for school. We had asked what happened. Everything seemed to be okay when we saw them less than a week ago for Thanksgiving.

He said they had an argument the night before which led to a little bit of push and shove. I thought I was going to go crazy. Here we are in New Jersey and they were down in Virginia. Hopefully, my son was still there.

Our phone calls were continuous throughout the night. Morning came and my nephew went to work as if it was just another day, except he put the dead bolt on the apartment door. It was about three o'clock in the afternoon when my nephew called, saying that he had just had the police over to report Billy missing and to report a break-in on his apartment. The door had been pushed through the frame since the dead bolt was locked. A gold chain was missing from his dresser. He had given all of Billy's information to the police officer, such as his social security number, his date of birth, and a recent picture. That was that ...we did not receive any more calls from him.

On Saturday there was a knock at the door. It was my nephew. He had an engagement party to go to up here in Jersey. We asked him about our son, and he said the cops would call if they heard anything. I could not believe this. He was up here while my son was somewhere down in Virginia. How could he be so irresponsible? I did not speak much to him for fear that I might lose it all. When he left, I told my husband that if we didn't hear anything by Monday night, I was going to Virginia on Tuesday and find my son.

The weekend seemed so long. I gave my son away and now he is missing, I thought. I had to stop feeling sorry for myself and straighten this mess out. I was determined to find my son. I called a program on television for missing children. A printer friend of the family made up a thousand missing posters for me. I went through the phone bill from when they were here on Thanksgiving and was able to get one of his girlfriend's phone numbers in Virginia. I also remember one close friend he spoke of, but I only knew his first name. I didn't know anyone else's last name.

Tuesday came and Billy was still missing. The detective did not find any information. In fact, they had not even started. One of my son's girlfriends from Jersey was coming with me to help play detective. My daughter and her friends put posters up in all of Monmouth County, just in case he somehow got a way back up here.

Well, we were off. We were about twenty minutes from my house when the van lost its gas pedal. It went right to the floor. I phoned my husband and he suggested I leave the next day. I told him no and to just bring me the truck, so he did. I guess there are sometimes when I can be aggressive. We were off again.

About six hours later we were at my nephew's apartment. He was there with his girlfriend. I first made a few phone calls, one to the police. It was then I found out that the detective handling the case was on partial disability, which meant he could not leave his desk. It also meant he started work at four PM and ended work at eight PM. He would never be able to go over to the school to find out the names and addresses of my son's friends, which meant he was pretty much useless. The other call was to the girlfriend, who at first said she knew nothing about my son's disappearance and did not know anybody's last name. However, when I got through with her she was giving me all kinds of information. So now I knew his best friend's last name and a general area in Virginia Beach where he lived. The other phone call was to my husband to let him know we arrived okay.

It was about six PM, and I asked my nephew to take us around to put out the fliers. I was shocked when he said he was going bowling and that if he found Billy he was going to give him a beating. That was the last straw. I began to scream, "We gave you four hundred dollars for the month of December to take care of our son. Since he hasn't been here take the four hundred dollars and fix your fucking door and buy another chain." That was just about our last words to each other. At least that's all I remember. My nephew's girlfriend showed us around some of the streets that night. We still slept at his apartment.

The next morning my partner and I went to school. They said they could not give us any information regarding a student's name or address. They said they could only give that information to the police, which we knew was impossible since the detective did not start work until after school was closed. After leaving the school, we made several stops putting fliers up in store front windows.

It was about two-thirty in the afternoon, and we decided to follow a couple of school buses. After following the bus to three stops we got lucky. We were in the right neighborhood. This one chubby boy came over to our truck after we called him. I asked him if he knew of my son's friend. I guess he really didn't care for him because he practically brought us to his front door.

I knocked, but nobody was home, so I left a missing flier with the neighbor. This neighbor said he had seen Billy a couple of days ago. We drove around that neighborhood for a couple of hours. Finally, there was a car parked outside his friend's house. A very thin woman opened the door in an old pink bathrobe that looked like an old bedspread. We could tell she was a heavy drinker and a hard worker. She had a southern accent. At the time though, she looked like an angel who was going to lead me to my son. She told me she saw Billy two nights ago when she had fed him dinner. I thought, good, at least he was eating. She then explained to me that she had been feeding him for the past month and that he only went home to my nephews to sleep. I wondered why he hadn't said any of this to me when we talked on the phone, or for that matter when I saw him two weeks ago. This woman still seemed like a vision to me. I was sure she would give me some answers. She mentioned that there was an apartment in the projects where this woman lived. All the boys would go there to party, but she wasn't sure where it was. We left with the understanding that she would get in touch with me if she heard anything.

While walking back to the truck, I said to my partner that I thought we were getting close. We both hoped so. While back at my nephew's apartment, I phoned the police station. I was actually giving them an update. He simply told me that when a kid is sixteen or older and missing, they want to be missing. So, they don't bother looking for them. Out of rage and frustration, I began to scream at him that this was my son out on the street. I asked him how he could be so inhuman. In my head, I was thinking they must be all inbreds in this town. From then on I knew if I didn't find my son, nobody was going to.

It was real dark now and my partner and I decided to stake out Billy's friend's house. I know that sounds funny now, but at the time it really wasn't. So here we sat with some munchies, soda, and cigarettes in a big dual-wheel, white pick-up. We had to make good with what we had. You know, we even had a few laughs. We felt just like Cagney and Lacey. Well, we had no action that night. We stayed until two AM and then decided to go back to the apartment for a couple of hours of sleep.

The next morning came bright and early. I was not playing any more games. We got up, stopped at the donut shop for something quick, and headed over to Billy's friend's neighborhood. Nothing at all seemed to be going on there so we then started driving around the projects. First of all, there has to be about a thousand units, and they all look alike. I decided to go to the manager's office. I was passed from one office to the next. Nobody would give me any answers. All I was asking was if there were any certain apartments that had complaints about them for having too many kids and too many parties. I guess they didn't want to ruin their reputation. We left there without any luck.

Then I got this bright idea and called the school and spoke with a southern accent. I said I was Billy's friend's mom and I wanted to know if he was in school today or if was he playing hooky again. Well, the attendance office informed me that he had not shown up for school. I left the phone booth and went directly over to Billy's friend's house and told his mother what I had done. She didn't seem at all surprised and said he was probably over at the projects. I was getting pretty sick of driving all around in that big white truck.

I went to the manager's office hoping to give it one more try, and it worked. This one woman felt so sorry for me that she gave me three apartment numbers. She said it had to be one of these. I also had to promise not to say where I got the information from. This was much better. We only had to circle three apartments instead of a thousand.

As we passed the third one, the blinds peeped open and closed. My partner said, "That's it! That's got to be the right one." Both of us, real brave, went up to the door, holding our breath. We knocked. A Spanish boy opened the door. I showed him my son's picture and asked if he had seen him. He said he thought he went back to New Jersey. Then my partner got really brave and asked for his friend by name. This must have thrown him off guard because he came to the door. He gave us the same story about Billy going back to New Jersey, so we left feeling real empty.

We went back to my nephew's apartment. From there I called the detective and told him I had found the apartment and asked if he could go there now. I told him I could smell the pot and there were beer cans all over the place. He said if he went there and didn't find anything, we wouldn't be able to go back again. He asked me if I had gone in and looked around and I told him no.

Then I asked if I was allowed to do that and he said it was worth a try.

So, we grabbed our bags and ran to the truck. We were only about twenty minutes away, but the twenty minutes were real scary as we wondered if they would let us in. We knew we were really close. I knocked at the door.

Once again, the Spanish boy answered and I asked if we could come in and look around. He said okay but wanted to know what we were looking for. I just replied, "My son."

We walked into what was supposed to be the living room. There was a television, a stereo, and two futons, without most of their cushions and cigarette butts stamped out into the carpet. The bedroom was worse mattress on the

floor and piles of dirty laundry up to our knees. There weren't any doors on the closets, so we knew he wasn't in there. I walked through the hallway, there was a closet with a fuse box in it and another closet that seemed to be painted shut. The bathroom I won't speak of. Then we came to the other bedroom, worse than the first. I couldn't believe all the dirty laundry. Again, no doors on the closets. There were a lot of blankets for many people to sleep on. There were about five more people there, too. Some were grown men.

It was really scary. The kitchen was empty. You could tell there wasn't any food there for quite a while. Well, it seemed like my son wasn't there. We were getting ready to leave and I said, "What the heck, I'll give it one more try." So I went back to that closet and I pulled with all my might, and guess who was pulling on the other side? My son. I was in complete shock.

There he was in the flesh, very thin, but still he was alive. Thank you, Jesus, I thought.

It wasn't all peachy. At first, he would not talk to me. Then we cried.

We took him and his friend to Roy Rogers and boy did they eat. When they were eating, I drove to a pay phone and called my husband. Before I told him anything I put Billy on. They talked for only a few minutes, made a couple of deals on the phone, and my son agreed to come home. We loaded up Billy's belongings from my nephew's place and we dropped his friend back off at the projects with a promise that Billy would see him again soon.

The drive home seemed like it took a lifetime. In the early part of the drive, Billy spoke of his adventure, if you will. He sold my nephew's chain and his beeper to eat, packaged sugar up, and sold it as drugs. He hadn't eaten in over a week and the apartment didn't have any heat, so it got pretty cold at night. The other five hours of the drive home he slept, and so did my partner since we really hadn't slept since Tuesday, and it was now Friday.

I drove home excited, proud, and exhausted. I just could not believe that was really me being aggressive and firm. I accomplished what I set out to do; I was bringing my son home for Christmas.

THIS IS A SURPRISE

One of the deals my husband made with Billy, in order for him to come home with me was that he could go back to Virginia Beach, to his friends for a visit. I said to my husband, "Why couldn't you say you were only kidding?" I knew just what the atmosphere was like there and I didn't want him going back, but my husband said he had made a deal and away we sent him on a bus, with an extra ticket for his friend to come back here and stay with us for a while.

Billy left on December twenty-seventh and was going to stay until about the fifth of January. He had called us every night as instructed. Well, the fifth came and my husband, my daughter, and I were patiently awaiting his arrival at the bus station in New York. The bus was about an hour late and I was becoming very nervous. All sorts of things were racing through my mind.

All I could do was remember that terrible apartment, the people, the dirt, and the drugs. I began praying, begging the Lord to make my son appear before me.

All of a sudden we saw Billy walking towards us. My daughter asked if his friend had long hair, and I said no. All three of us were standing there with our mouths wide open. There he was, standing with this girl. Nobody said anything, so I broke the ice. "Where did she come from?" Billy said, "Virginia." I said,

"Where is she going?" "Our house." My husband just picked up the suitcase and began walking to the elevators. My son and this girl followed him. Sharon and I were bringing up the rear.

As we were walking to the elevator, Sharon leaned into me and in a hushed voice said, "This is a surprise." I thought to myself, it certainly was, to say the least. We were all speechless.

We got into the elevator and my husband said in a very low voice, "She better not be a runaway."

"Oh, she's not," my son replied. Not a word was spoken in the sixty- minute ride home. We stopped at a restaurant in our town because we thought that they might be hungry. It turned out they hadn't eaten for about a day.

Still, nothing was mentioned about the girl.

So, once again I had to play detective. First I called Virginia and spoke to the boy's mom, that is, the boy who was supposed to come home with my son. I found out she knew where my son was the whole time he was missing– some angel in a faded pink bathrobe. Anyway, I called her hoping to get some answers. I found out the girl's name and also that she had run away from home about a week ago. In the meantime, her family had moved. Well, wasn't this getting exciting? I thought. The only way I was going to solve this was to get close to her and become her friend.

I thought this was going to take some time, but I was wrong. She was a very lonely girl and wanted to be loved.

Billy got very angry with us when we told him she wasn't sleeping in his room. After about a week, Billy lost interest in her. Instead, he brought home a shepherd-type puppy and asked if he could keep him. We said yes. It was much easier letting him keep a puppy than keeping a girl... This puppy was to be named Mookie, and would later become my pride and joy.

Now it was like I had another daughter, I really enjoyed having her around. As time passed, I was able to pick up bits and pieces, such as, her father was in high command in the service, stationed in Virginia. I also found out her last name. I got in touch with the army base, only to find out that her father had been transferred to another part of Virginia. After several phone calls and going through all different levels of the service, I was able to locate her father, or should I say, stepfather. He really didn't want her back.

She really was a good kid. She had a very hard life, and it was already catching up with her. She had been at our house then for a few weeks. At this point, she had no reason to lie about anything. All she wanted was someone to love and care for her. After about a month of having her company, her father called and said her aunt would take her to Maryland. The only thing was that he told his daughter she had found her way back to New

Jersey, so she should find her way to Maryland. How do you think that child felt? First, her family doesn't want her, then somehow she is supposed to find a way from New Jersey to Maryland I felt he was a heartless bastard. My husband and I could not send a sixteen-year-old girl alone on a bus for a four-hour ride. Needless to say, I took her to her aunt's in Maryland. By this time I seemed to be capable of doing almost anything. That would be the last time I would see that young lady. I did receive one letter and a phone call. She said that our closeness and the long talks we had made a definite impression on her, and she thanked me for it.

OUR FIRST TRY AT

REHABILITATION

It was February now and we were trying to enroll Billy back in high school. It was very difficult. They did not want him back. They made him sign all types of contracts. For instance, if he was suspended, that was it—he was out. He lasted about two weeks. Again, he was in more trouble and yes, it was drug-related.

We were able to get him in a Federally Funded program in Secaucus. We brought him and all his belongings to the rehab. He was in there for two days when we went there for Family Day. He seemed to be adjusting and communicating with some of the other adolescents, he just wasn't communicating with us. We were the enemy. The counselors explained that a lot of them are like that and that he would come around in time. We left with little hope.

The next night, at about nine PM, we got a phone call from the facility in Secaucus. The woman informed us that our son had escaped. The alarms had been sounded and the doors locked. The police had been signaled. We, of course, jumped in the car and sped all the way there. There was complete silence in the car. My heart was racing. All I kept thinking was, oh God, don't let this happen again. The ride usually took an hour...we were there in forty-five minutes. We went directly to the office. The woman said the police had not yet found him, but they almost always do. She continued by saying, "When they do find him, you're going to have to take him home because once they run away, we don't take them back." We weren't worrying about bringing him back, we just wanted to find him. At that moment the police called. Billy had turned himself in. We picked him up and drove home. Again, there wasn't much conversation, just a small sigh of relief.

Later, when we got home, there were three messages on the answering machine. All of them were from Billy. He was begging us to come and get him. He was freezing, he had no coat and no idea where he was. He just wanted to come home. My heart ached listening to the tape... I saved it to remind him, but sometime later he destroyed it.

That was our first attempt at rehabilitating our son. I put my foot down and said if he wasn't going to school, he would have to get his GED.

The community college was having classes for the high school equivalency test, but as usual, there was always a problem. Because my son was on probation and because the charge involved a weapon, they did not want him in their school. I asked the director of the program, rather I begged her, to let him just take the test. I knew he would pass. She had me sign the papers waiving the classes and gave him a test date.

About a week later, I dropped him off at the college to take the test. He met up with a friend who had finished the classes and was also taking the test.

Billy completed the test and gave all the answers to his friend. It took about two months when us got his diploma in the mail. So did his friend. It still would be very difficult to get a job, even though he had a diploma. He was only sixteen. This meant he had a lot of free time on his hands to get into a lot more trouble.

Sharon, on the other hand, was much more relieved knowing her brother wasn't going to be in her school anymore. She could now have her own identity. She was now dating the boy she spoke of in November on the ride home from Virginia. They were going on five months of continuous phone conversations when they weren't seeing each other. She was in love and so was he.

It was also about this time that my daughter kept bugging me to take her to a fortune teller, or someone in that type of field. I knew she was looking for answers. I'm not sure if it was about her future or the past, but whatever she was looking for, she wasn't going to find it that night. Instead, I got an ear full.

The girl we went to had been a numerologist. She was also the sister of my first boyfriend, prior to my marriage. Even though she hadn't spoken with me in more than seventeen years, she could read me like a book. Or should I say, she could see right through me.

She first spoke with my daughter, and basically gave her all good news, but nothing deep into the future. My daughter was very disappointed, to say the least. Then it was my turn, this girl did all she could do not to cry or make me cry, and this was before she did the thing with the numbers. She said my vibes were so strong that she could feel all my depression. Mind you, before I went there, I made sure I looked perfect and perky.

She said that a few times when she had seen me around, she had experienced the same feelings without speaking to me. In fact, that was why she did not return my calls for an appointment for two months. I only went to her to find out about our financial problems, which now seemed to be the least of my problems. She mentioned my son and saw him being institutionalized. But she did say that someday he would be the person that I would be proud of, but not for a while. Then there was the issue of my mother, who I hadn't spoken to in more than ten years. She was very sick, which I was aware of, but how did the fortune teller know all this? She informed me that it was only a matter of months before she wasn't going to be with us anymore. She felt that I should make amends before it was too late, or I would never forgive myself.

The other issue was my state of mind, which I thought was in a pretty good state. But boy, did she pull some things out of those numbers. Maybe some of what she said was because she didn't care for my husband, or maybe she really could see what was going on in my head. I wasn't going to let her know that I blamed a lot of what my son was going through on his father and that there was much resentment towards him at the time. So, when she asked if I did anything for myself as enjoyment, I told her I was writing a book. Her advice to me was to continue putting it into words.

After all this co-called spiritual advice, I began to change. I'm not sure what exactly was changing, but it was something inside which I could not control. I became bitter towards my husband, and I know if I had all these resentful feelings steaming inside of me then my son must have been boiling up. I was determined to turn this thing around once again. My love for my family was much stronger than the bitterness that was trying to control me.

REUNITED WITH MY MOTHER

What my friend, the numerologist had said was really beginning to eat at me. It wasn't me who had initiated the silence between me and my mother, but I never tried to break it for ten years. In the beginning, it was really difficult, especially around the holidays. But as the years passed, I missed my family less and less. It seemed all senseless now that she was so ill. Even though I became very close to my stepmother, though she wasn't my biological mother, she certainly was my logical mother, and I loved her dearly. Something inside me still wanted to speak to my real mother before it would be too late. Every so often my brother, the only one who did speak to me, would call and tell me how she was doing. She had a bad heart, bad lungs, and osteoporosis—all her bones were breaking. I was able to send a letter to her in Florida through a friend. I didn't let my husband know because I didn't want to hurt him either. They had all stopped talking to me because of him. I never knew if she got the letter.

This was the letter:

Dear Mom,

I have to write you this letter to tell you I am not one bit angry with you. You did what any mom would do for her daughter. I am writing you to tell you I am OK and have never been hit since the day you were here. I always think of you and pray to God for Him to let you know I love you. Bill doesn't know I am writing this letter. I think it's just best that way. The kids are pretty grown up now. Lil' Billy is a big problem...kind of like his father. Drugs and alcohol. We are seeking professional help. He really is a beautiful young man. He's very smart but doesn't care to be smart in school. He's tall for this family, 5' 10". Now Sharon is another story. She's everything I ever wanted to be. She's great in school, very beautiful and very popular. One thing, she's very short. 5'0". Here are their most recent pictures.

I've been through a lot in the past 10 years. Most of the time I seem to not feel too well. I had three miscarriages, the last one was a big surgery. I had hernia surgery, the worst was, that I had Lymes Disease for almost three years. I was real sick, but after a year and a half of IV, I seemed to be ok. It's been about one year since I've been sick. I guess that's because I need all my strength to help my son through his problems.

I'm sorry to hear that you're not feeling well. I hope you will feel better soon. All my prayers are with you...can you feel them? Please, Mom, know that you're in my heart.

I love you, Your daughter, Cheryl.

Finally, one day I told my husband I really wanted to get in touch with her. He agreed that it was the best thing for me. I was happy to have his approval. I was getting ready to plan a trip to

Florida when my friend, the messenger, came over for a visit. He then told me that my mother was right here in New Jersey with her sister. I built up all my courage and dialed my aunt's phone number. I heard a little voice answer the phone, "Hello, hello?" I hung up. I told my husband I would see him later and he wished me luck.

On the drive over, I was extremely anxious. All types of things were running through my mind. Would she be angry to see me? I stopped at a local bakery and picked up some cookies. I thought it was the proper thing to do. I was driving down my aunt's street and I actually went right past her house. I turned around and parked right in front. I walked up to the porch, fixing my hair, hoping she would like what she saw. I rang the bell and waited. A little voice kept saying, "I'm coming." Just then the door opened. She said, "Can I help you?"

I said, "Don't you know me?" She asked if I was one of the neighbor's daughters. I then said, "It's me, mom, Cheryl." Well, I had to reach in before she nearly fell backward. There was this tiny, white-haired older woman that I could hardly recognize. She had been hooked up to the oxygen, which was why it had taken her so long to come to the door. Her cheeks were puffy from all the medications she was on. Ten years ago she was about five foot, two inches. Now I bet she wasn't more than four feet eleven. Her bones had disintegrated unbelievably.

She began to hug and kiss me. I couldn't have gotten away if I tried. She cried and said her prayers were answered, and that there wasn't anything else she wanted from life. We sat down and began to talk. I told her all about my children since she had missed all their growing-up years. She never mentioned the past, only that she had received my letter and took it with her wherever she went. Our visit went on for five hours. I don't know where the time went, but it was the most beautiful reunion I could ever have asked for.

My contact with her has remained. I make sure I see her at least once a week and I have phone conversations regularly. And, once again, I must split my holidays up so that I get to see both my father and his wife and my mother.

But that's no big deal, I'm pretty good at that.

A DARK CLOUD

It was April and my daughter was going to turn fifteen on the twelfth. But a black cloud shadowed the month of April, as early as the eighth. My daughter's best friend was killed in a car accident on prom night. He was only seventeen. My daughter was devastated. We knew him very well. He would always stop over to say Hi and have macaroni with us. He and my daughter had a special kind of love, the closest two best friends there could be. Sharon's boyfriend understood this entirely and was there to comfort her with all his heart.

The funeral was the largest I have ever seen, I'll bet over three thousand attended. The church and parking lot were completely packed. I never saw so many kids comfort and mourn together. There was a group of over two hundred children that met night after night at the accident site with candles doing spiritual vigils with the priest from our parish. The girl that was his date was in a coma for about two weeks. All the children collected their money and bought groceries for her family. I'll tell you; God was shining down on all those children.

One sad thing at that very large funeral was that there was one person missing...my son. I know it was not out of disrespect that he was not there, but more out of fear. You see, he had not stepped foot in a church in well over a year. I know deep in my heart that he just would not have been able to handle anything like this at this time in his life. So, he broke it off by saying that he felt bad for the boy but that we all had to go some time.

Sharon's birthday was on the twelfth, which was the day her friend was to be buried. She had asked us not to celebrate or even mention it, so we respected her wishes.

Things got pretty hectic after that. We were being very lenient with my daughter as far as going out. You see, it was very hard to talk to her without her crying. One day around four in the afternoon, she said she was going to the boardwalk, so my husband gave her twenty dollars. He was getting ready to go to the racetrack. Billy said, "How about me?" with his hand out. Now mind you, we knew that any money we gave to him would end up going to pot and beer. My husband only handed him five dollars.

Well, that's when the shit hit the fan. Billy became this raging maniac, kind of like the one I used to see in my husband years ago. He began to scream, "Who does he think he is, giving me five and her twenty?" I saw fire in his eyes and the language was unbelievable. He punched holes in the doors and walls. Things were flying from room to room. I don't know how many times he said he hated his father, but it was several. He kept saying how he wanted to kill him. Then he would go into the goriest details and he would speak at how he would laugh as he was hurting and killing his father. Chills ran up and down my spine. I just thanked God my husband wasn't there at the time because I knew there would have been bloodshed. After all these years I knew I had to tell my husband how my son felt whether it hurt his feelings or not. I had to get in touch with him to warn him. I finally got him, but he blew it off by saying the kid was full of hot air. My husband just didn't understand that the problem had to be met and dealt with. It really didn't faze him one way or the other. At least I felt better not keeping anything to myself.

Once again, we had to go to court for our son. I was beginning to share him with my husband. Our son violated his probation by coming up positive in one of his urine tests. We knew it was going to happen sooner or later. I was just getting sick and tired of going to court. I wrote a letter to the judge.

Although I never gave it to him, it helped me to have the strength to do what I had to do:

Your Honor,

We cannot be responsible for our son as he does whatever he wants, whenever he wants. We cannot make sure he reports when he is supposed to. We never know where he is or how to get in touch with him. If we ground him, he sneaks out at night. We tried taking shifts, (my husband and I), staying up all night. After three nights, we gave up. We took away his phone, so he now goes across the street to the pay phone. We do not give him any money. He must get it from his friends. We haven't bought him anything except tooth paste, soap, and food. I will not allow my husband to hit him, for fear that DYFS will come and take our daughter away.

He has no respect for us as adults or parents. We have to hide money and jewelry because he steals from us. He curses and swears at me and breaks up my house. His room is like a disgusting slum–filthy clothes, old food, and cigarettes all over the floor. There is broken furniture. It's a real shame. He has no respect for anyone, including himself. He acts like we owe him something. Well, we are finished giving. We are also finished taking abuse. If we have to put up with it until he is eighteen we will. But then, all his belongings, and him, are out.

Yours truly, Cheryl Costello

For the second time, my son had to go to a rehabilitation facility and stay there. Otherwise, the next stop was the juvenile hall. We knew he didn't want to go there. He agreed to go wherever our insurance sent him. It didn't matter if he had agreed or not–he was going. This time it was way up in the mountains in Pennsylvania. There was no running away this time.

The letters we received were much more civilized. Could this really be working, or did he finally find out how to play their minds too? I wondered.

Meanwhile, Sharon had been very busy with her Honors English Class. She had been chosen from several entrants for an Oratorical contest which was sponsored by the Optimist Club. She remained after school for several days rehearsing her speech. When I asked her if I could hear it, she said wait until the big night. This wasn't like her; she had always asked me to listen to her poems and such. But I respected her wishes and waited for the big night.

She also asked that only I attend. She said she really didn't want her father to be there. I didn't have any idea why she said this, but he was probably happy not to attend the school function anyway. It just wasn't his style.

The day before the big night, she and her boyfriend had a big fight. That's one thing she never discussed with me. She couldn't go to school because all she did was cry. My heart ached for her. There was nothing I could do or say that would help her feel better. In fact, I sat and cried with her. The big day was here. She got up and went to school, leaving several classes because she couldn't keep the tears back. Her English teacher tried to talk to her, but it wasn't any use. Sharon didn't think she would be able to make the speech. After school, her boyfriend brought her a rose and straightened a lot of things out. They were still going to the prom in May. She felt much better and began picking out something to wear for the speech that night.

Sharon and I went to the hotel where the awards were being held. I sat close up front so I could hear her completely. Her teacher was sitting behind me with a box of tissues which I didn't see. It was my daughter's turn and I was all ears.

She began:

"Listen To Me...

I understand that our audience has a variety of people here tonight, although what I'm about to say is mainly directed at teenagers. So, I would like to ask all of the teenagers to pay extra attention and really listen to what I have to say.

Listen to me I believe that being a teenager today you have to be your own person. Today's youth are leaders, not followers. Our determination is incredible, and all of us are role models for others.

We are capable of making our own decisions concerning positive issues such as higher education and ecological preservation, and voicing our opinions. Us teenagers have the blunt talent of saying what we want, when we want. If we have something on our minds we're not afraid of sharing it whether it be good or bad. Now you're probably all thinking, "Well, what's so great about that?" If it's only to an extent and doesn't hurt anyone's feelings, that is a terrific characteristic. Only a few short years ago certain issues were understood not to be brought up, issues such as homosexuality and racism. Today's youth are openly aware of these topics because of our curiosity and the fact that if we have a question we're not afraid of asking it.

Another terrific attribute of the youth of today is our determination. We know what we want and we don't stop until we get it. Now I'm positive that all of the parents can relate to this situation. How many

times has a child asked to do something and their parent flat out said no and insisted that was the end of it? Then, after about an hour or pleading and crying, topped off with a dab of guilt, they gave in.

That's just one everyday example proving our persistence.

Now I have a message for all of my peers. I want all of you teenagers to listen to me very carefully. I really, truly hope you all understand how much each and every one of you is looked up to. We are all leaders therefore we have responsibilities. Try to think back to when you were in second and third grade. Do you remember the big kids and do you remember how badly you wanted to be one of them? Well, that's just what you are now. You are a role model for every child younger than you, often including your peers. They want to look like you, talk like you, and even walk like you. All in all, they want to be just like you. Children are so impressionable, so please, please don't lead them in the wrong direction. I grew up with my parents and my older brother. My brother is only two years older than me, so of course we were always very close. I went to him for advice, opinions, and guidance. He as always there to stand up for me and never let anyone hurt me. I was his baby sister. So no doubt about it, I trusted him more than anyone. My brother, my role model, is presently in rehab. He is a narcotic user as well as an alcoholic. A few years ago I never imagined he would do anything to hurt me. I used to smoke, he gave me my first cigarette. I used to drink, and that first drink came from the same place also. Thank God and my parents that I've learned to learn from his mistakes before I followed too far in his footsteps. All I am trying to get across is please don't lead others in the wrong direction. I looked up at my brother, now I look down on him. I don't feel that anyone wants to be looked down upon, so please don't let it happen.

My last message to you is to remember, that if you can set your goals and not be distracted by peer pressure, you can achieve anything you choose The world is an open opportunity for everyone. So take pride in your choices and strive for them. We are the hope for the future."

When she finished, there wasn't a dry eye in the house. No wonder she couldn't rehearse with me ahead of time, or that she didn't want her father there. You see, she said it perfectly. If her father was there she would have been crying also. She says her daddy always makes her cry. We would have become a very emotional family. God bless my daughter to be able to see through all this mess and to find strength through it. She won first prize for her speech.

The letters continued from our son. We had received a phone call from his counselor. He assured me that my son was improving tremendously. He was sharing in the group and participating in activities. He felt that Billy was ready for some open counseling with his family, especially with his father. I felt this was the perfect opportunity for my husband to get reacquainted with his son. I was sure that the only way this was going to be straightened out was if the two of them got together with a middleman, anyone but me. I was lucky because at that time I had a horse at home that was due to give birth, so I used that as an excuse not to go. This way it was just my son and my husband. It sounded good at the time, but I don't think much came of the meeting. I think they both chickened out. Billy was turning seventeen in May. Since he did hold up his end of the agreement by not running away from the rehab, my husband decided to buy him his first car. Since we were in the business, we had some contacts. Bill was able to purchase a 1980, 924 Porsche, cheap. It needed some work. Originally it was white, but Billy wanted a black car, so we painted the car and changed the interior. I'll tell you, it was a real head turner just what he was looking for.

My husband brought Billy home with all his literature and programs he was supposed to follow. It was good to see him. He looked much healthier. It was a week before his birthday, I handed him a little wrapped box and said, "Happy Birthday!" He opened it and there was a key on a Porsche key ring.

He said, "You got me a car? What kind?"

We said, "Look at the key ring." He looked at it and said, "No way." He ran out to the garage screaming, "I got a Porsche." I guess you could say he was excited.

THE TRAILER

Billy was seventeen and a half now and totally out of control. He would go out at night and stay away for days. All the yelling and screaming did nothing. Sometimes he would work—believe me, he could get those manual jobs easily. He was big and had quite a bit of muscle, and those construction companies loved to hire strong kids and pay them half of that they would a trained man. He started up the fall semester at a local community college. We could tell from the start he really wasn't interested, but he had his shiny little black Porsche, so he was ready and willing to go to maybe pick up a few girls. I guess that's all that's on a seventeen-year-old boy's mind.

The school only lasted about seven weeks, and we began to get notices for unattended classes. That was the end of college.

One morning my husband and I got up to go for breakfast, one thing we always did together for the past eighteen. Go to a diner for breakfast. It was nice to have a little time to ourselves each day. As we were getting into the car, we discussed the terrible storm that had lasted all night. But most importantly, there wasn't any Porsche in the driveway. I kind of had the witchy feeling—the kind of feeling when you know something bad happened. I hoped my son was all right.

Later that afternoon while I was at a luncheon with my daughter, my husband got a phone call from Billy. He asked his father to send a tow truck, he had an accident around 3:00 A.M. this morning and he didn't think the car could be driven. He said that he and three other friends who were in the car had pushed it off the road after hitting a tree. Everyone was okay. No injuries, no police.

My husband sent the tow truck. Meanwhile, I came home and he told me about Billy calling. It was three hours since the call and neither the car nor my son had shown up yet. Right then we heard the chains on the truck outside. The driver was surprised that anyone had even survived the accident. The only thing salvageable was the hood emblem. There wasn't any body panel that hadn't been crushed. We were in a state of shock. Now we were waiting to see our son. He came home about an hour later and he was right, nobody was hurt. I guess that it's true when they say God watches over babies and drunks, and you know which category they fell into. They were lucky not to have the police involved, as we were since it was insured in our name. We only had liability on it, so it was hooked back up to the tow truck and dropped off at the junkyard. I kept the emblem for sentimental reasons.

This would not be the only car my son totaled. Within one year of driving, he totaled three cars. Not all were because of drinking some were mostly out of stupidity.

Billy continued to work at many different jobs. He was always complimented on how well he did with whatever it was they had him do. But as soon as they showed some type of authority, he would quit. He always took the easy way out. Both he and my husband would just sort of pass each other in the house. There wasn't a lot of speaking going on. You see, my husband was also a slightly bit childish and quick to pick an argument, and then in the next minute he would hand Billy a twenty-dollar bill, I guess this was because he felt guilty, or maybe it was his only way to show him love. All I knew was that it was pissing me off. This didn't help in showing him any responsibility.

I came up with a bright idea...putting a mobile home up on the back part of our property. This seemed to have many benefits. Billy would learn some responsibility because he would have to pay rent and take care of his own place. So my husband and I go over to this trailer park and purchase, what could be considered a condemned trailer. We hooked it up to our truck, thinking there shouldn't be any problem pulling it home, about ten miles. Boy, were we in for a surprise? First, we blew two tires on the trailer while on the road and had to change them in the dark. You see, we had to move it in the dark so that the township didn't know exactly what we were doing. All this for my disrespectful, irresponsible, and ungrateful son. But I loved him to death.

We finally got the trailer into position on our property. My husband borrowed a backhoe, dug the septic, and ran the electricity. I cleaned for two weeks. Finally, we had a beautiful little home in our back yard. That was actually the last time that it was going to be beautiful.

Billy and his friends moved in with all good intentions. They both paid their rent up front and Billy was planning on going back to college. We didn't see much of him, but if we drove over to the side of the property, we would see his car. It was kind of a relief. He always seemed to be in his home. At least now he was safe. If he or his friends did drink, they would just crash there instead of driving home. I use the word 'crash', because that was exactly what they did. Several kids were making themselves comfortable in my son's house. He didn't mind, but it was beginning to eat at me. The furniture, the carpet, the blinds, and the curtains were destroyed. About once a week he would clean the place up, filling the large dumpster we had with trash. Most of it was beer cans. Then he would bring his laundry to me, about six loads a week. I should really say everybody's laundry. I had this phobia, you might say...I loved to do laundry. I wouldn't let anyone touch my washer or dryer.

I used them so much that I was on my fifth set since we were married eighteen years ago. I used to be so particular with Billy's clothes. I hung all of his shirts so that they didn't shrink. But that wasn't the case anymore. I was washing, drying, and shrinking everybody's clothes and it felt good.

All this activity...the party life...went on for about seven months. Yes, my son did start college again. And yes, he did quit again. We were not surprised. At this point, nothing surprised us. The last four months of their stay were a nightmare. The cars were up and down the driveway all night long. Nobody had a job and there hadn't been any rent paid for months. And now Billy was coming home every day to eat. I didn't mind feeding him, but all the food he would take back to feed the others got on my nerves.

Finally, I put my foot down. We were evicting them. We told Billy that he was welcome to move back to his old room, but he had to live by some of our rules. The party was over. It started out to be a good idea, but like many ideas, it backfired. So, home again he was.

SWEET SIXTEEN AND COMING OF

AGE

It was senior prom weekend. Even though Billy wasn't graduating with his class, he was going to make sure he didn't miss the parties they were having down at the shore. He left on a Friday night and said he would see us in a couple of days. All I said to him was to be careful. Prom nights always seem to have something happen. He didn't call us, but I didn't expect him to. Saturday morning came and my husband and I were still sleeping. I heard the front door open. I asked, "Who is it?" My son announced it was him. I knew something had to be wrong for him to come home a day early.

He came in front of the bedroom door and all I could see was his entire forearm professionally wrapped up. It seemed that a big fight had broken out in the hotel where they were staying, and somehow Billy had put his arm through a window. The blood began to squirt across the room, he had nicked a main artery. The fight broke up when everybody saw the blood and he was rushed to the emergency room with a police escort. He and his friends who went to the hospital with him were not charged with anything. All the others were. They thought they were so lucky, but the lucky one was my son. He had just turned eighteen and was able to sign for them to do immediate treatment. He had lost a lot of blood. His friends had actually thought he was going to die. Thank God once again for watching over him, I thought.

Billy still worked, but couldn't seem to find a stable job or one that he was going to be happy with. Sharon, on the other hand, worked all hours as a waitress. She was a real hustler when it came to making money. She was also very generous and helpful to me.

We had just finished celebrating her big bash. It was her sweet sixteen birthday. You wouldn't believe what she put me through in order to pull off the most perfect party. First, we had to look for hotels to cater to it. We went to about five or six when she finally found one she liked. It was because of the picture over the fireplace. She just loved the Victorian style. That wasn't too hard. Then we had to pick out perfect invitations, which took hours. From there we went to get favors. She decided we should make them, the ones that are made inside of balloons. It wasn't easy making sixteen of them the morning before the party.

The hardest thing to find was her gown. She wanted to be the most elegant and outstanding among all the rest. I would have to say, and not due to the fact that she was my daughter, she was the most beautiful girl in the entire building. Talk about making two parents proud.

The couple of hours prior to the party were frantic, but that's how everything with Sharon was. First, we dropped everything off at the hotel. There were over a hundred balloons. They were mauve and pearl white with ribbons hanging from them. We had to fill them there at the hotel, my daughter and me. We put all the centerpieces on the table. The room looks so beautiful, I thought. She felt there weren't enough balloons.

From there we went to get her hair done. She was getting it all put up with pearls around the crown of her head. This took quite a while. Then we picked up some lavender balloons, about seventy-five, and we rushed home. I still had to get dressed and do my hair. Thank goodness it was curly at the time, so I was real quick. Then we all proceeded to blow the balloons up with the helium and tie the ribbons on them. It was me, my husband, and my son. Billy looked really handsome in his suit. His hair was pretty long but he had it slicked back. I guess you could say we had the two best-looking kids there.

Anyway, we got into three cars—with that many balloons we needed at least three cars--and we arrived at the hotel in just enough time to release the seventy-five balloons to the ceiling and collect ourselves. The party was perfect. The food was excellent. Sharon's speeches were out of this world. Thank God every so often we have a few good times like this to remember and enjoy. Her one special gift was Shabi, a Pekinese.

We celebrated our nineteenth wedding anniversary. It wasn't any different from the other eighteen—we never celebrated holidays anymore. Only Christmas and that was because of the children. They were the light of my life, just as they were in the early years. I still spent all my time thinking about my son and running all over creation for my daughter.

We had a barbeque in the yard for Billy's eighteenth birthday. It was a combination party—half for his birthday and half for receiving his GED. I kind of felt bad not being able to have a graduation party for him. The day came and went and everything was back to normal, at least for our family. Billy was still staying out nights, but nobody came over to our house, meaning his friends. He cleaned his act up a little bit. He took a test at the racetrack and became a teller. The one big problem he had was that he was just like me. He hated the racetrack and the people that went along with it. He would come home every day so frustrated. His father thought the job was great, but he loved everything about the track. They were definitely two different people when it came to the race business. Against my better judgment, I agreed to let my husband get involved with the horse business only because he didn't have any hobbies since he gave up drinking. I was raised in the horse business and had very little to do with it because of that. Once again, we were falling into that position.

Billy did manage to save enough money to get his own car insurance.

He did have many points, so his insurance was extremely high. We were repairing an Acura which we were going to sell. Billy made a deal with his father to pay one hundred dollars a week until the car was paid for. This all sounded excellent, but it never happened. His insurance was raised another thousand for an accident that wasn't his fault. He was making a left turn into our driveway when a township water truck attempted to pass him on the driver's side. The township police officer did not issue a ticket to the truck driver as it was a friend of his. Billy was rushed to the hospital for what turned out to be a chip off his spinal column. Billy also received five points from the insurance company for receiving medical attention. The cards were beginning to stack against him.

At this time, Sharon was beginning to not feel so well. Her throat had become swollen, almost closed. She was running a fever and her head hurt so bad she couldn't lift it off the pillow. While in the emergency room, the doctors had us scared to death. Immediately they tested her for spinal meningitis and gave her an antibiotic shot right in the butt. Then they told us to bring her back right away if she got a fever, a rash, or if she could not move her neck. I drove home trying not to let her know how nervous I was. She was crying, saying she didn't want to die. Later that night, she told me she had a rash on her hands. By this time she was so paranoid. I could not see any rash. She insisted she could feel it. The next morning, she woke up screaming. Her entire body was covered in a red, raised rash.

We rushed back to the hospital. They took one look at her and said the rash was a reaction to the antibiotic, which meant she had something other than spinal meningitis. She had mono. Oh, what a relief, I thought. We could deal with this. Dealing with Mono wasn't as easy as I thought it would be.

She was tired and weak for several months. She had to quit her job, quit the gym, and quit dancing. For me, it was a break from driving her all around, but for her, it was like the world came to a complete stop. She also had a pageant coming up in November which she had to prepare for. This was no small-town pageant, it was the Miss New Jersey Teen U.S.A. Pageant. There were nearly eighty contestants. Again, things were going to be hectic.

Two weeks before the pageant, we went to the hotel for orientation.

When we left there her wheels were spinning. We had everything we needed, or so I thought. She decided to change her mind – a new gown, new business suit, new bathing suit. She had to be pleased or there was no living with her.

I know she sounds spoiled and maybe she was, but she gave us everything we asked for. She showed us respect, responsibility, and unconditional love. Her grades were outstanding. What more could a parent want from their child? So, we spent the next two weeks running from store to store. Actually, this type of pace is what I lived for.

THE TURNING POINT

My son did not want to go to the pageant which was all well and good because my daughter really didn't want him there. He decided to take a ride to some college in Maryland with his girlfriend and a male friend of his. They were going to stay there for a couple of days.

It seems that he had an argument with his girlfriend and left Maryland in a hurry without both of his friends. He was driving his 1990 Acura which was bright red. This little car could really move– he was clocked at 98 miles per hour on the New Jersey Turnpike by a state trooper. Well, there went his license for at least three months, since he was on probation. He was having a tough time paying for the car and his insurance before. This was going to be the straw that broke the camel's back.

Another dramatic event happened while Billy was in Maryland. His best friend, the one I believe tarnished my son, finally got locked up. Of course, it was not anything to do with drugs. He always had a way of getting all of his drug charges dropped. This time it was something really serious. He was arrested for some type of assault charge. All I do know is that Billy thought he would be going away for a couple of years.

This must have felt like the end of the world to my son. He wouldn't have a license, so he wouldn't have a job. Now he couldn't pay for his car and most of all he didn't have his best friend around anymore. For three days he seemed to pace frantically through the house. Anger seemed to fill him and he was ready to blow at any time. All he kept saying to me was, "What am I going to do?" Then he said, "Get me the number of the Marines."

My heart began to pound. I said to myself, "Oh, God, please don't make this a dream. Please let him follow through with this rage." I got him the number as soon as I could, but I would not call for him. I felt that this was his decision. Besides, I didn't want him to say later that I made him do it. He called and got an appointment for the next day.

That night, my husband, my daughter, and I were out to dinner when we saw a friend. I remembered that his son had already enlisted in the Marines, so I told my husband to go over and ask when he was leaving. It turns out he wasn't leaving until January. This was great. Maybe they could both go in on the "buddy system." Only to find out they wouldn't accept him with only a GED he was getting shot down one more time.

His friend who was already enlisted took him to meet his staff Sergeant.

I made a few phone calls and found out that he could go to night school and request the test in advance. If he passed all the tests, all thirteen of them, he would receive a high school diploma. These thirteen tests counted for the sixty-five credits he needed to pass high school.

Once again, I became a super mom. I had to organize, supervise, chauffeur, and become a student again. This was the week before Thanksgiving, so I also had to plan dinner for my dad and my logical mother.

Eight of my son's tests were completed before Thanksgiving. With the help of many people, he received 'A's and two 'B's. At Thanksgiving dinner, my son announced to his grandparents that he had enlisted in the Marines. My father was so proud that he just glowed. We gave thanks that my son began to see the light. It was still very dim, but he did see it.

The next two weeks he studied endlessly. He had a math test, which would be no problem, two English tests, which would be some problem, and a history test which would be an extreme problem. For two weeks all I did was help him study. I think I did more than I did when I was in high school. In between studying, I prayed—that special Novena to Baby Jesus is some powerful stuff.

I kept telling the teachers he was extremely smart. So in the nick of time, he had the papers he needed for the Marines and he would now be able to leave with his friend on January 13th.

It was now December 18th and I had just enough time to prepare for Christmas. Talk about being excited and scared at the same time. It's kind of a sickening feeling. Christmas was here and gone. My daughter was very depressed. At first, I thought maybe she didn't get enough for Christmas, but then her true colors began to show. She seemed very jealous of her brother, but actually, it wasn't that.

You see, all her life she was the one in the spotlight. Everything she did sparkled. She was so special, so perfect, yet so invisible at this moment that she just didn't understand what was happening. She just finished in the top ten in a very large pageant and had been inducted into the National Honors Society. Her grades were excellent. She shouted between her tears, "He's not smoking pot because he can't. He's drinking every night. He borrows your last dollar. He borrows money to buy you a Christmas gift. I don't smoke, I don't drink, I get straight 'A's. I cashed my bonds to buy your Christmas gifts, and you borrow money to give to him."

Well, she was right about every single thing she said. It was just something I couldn't explain. I told her that this situation was like the Prodigal Son. My son had seen the light. I told her I did appreciate everything she did and I was sorry I took her for granted. I tried to explain that I loved them both and that they were both part of me, just going in different directions. After a couple of days, she seemed to be more like herself again.

THE THIRTEEN WEEKS

I knew then that blessing number one was really leaving. My husband kept saying he would be back. I knew he would be back, but it wasn't ever going to be the same again. I wasn't going to be the one to help him make his decisions or try to control his life. I say the word 'try' because Lord knows there was no controlling Billy.

What was really ironic about this whole thing was that having my son around for the past two months was great. He became so much more family-oriented. He would sit around the table with us after dinner just to talk. He actually cleaned the fridge out and organized the closets. Why couldn't this have happened four years ago? I wondered. Now, we only had two short months to enjoy him. Well, thank God it happened at all. At least now he was really finding himself, and that person he was finding was really special.

The day before Billy left, a close friend of his came over with a going-away gift. It was a bible. I said to myself, "I hope he doesn't smoke that one like he did the last one he had." I decided to go into my son's room before he left just to see what mess was in store for me. The first thing I saw was the bible had been unwrapped. I began to look through it and there, written in the proper places, were all our family names. My son actually filled in all the spaces. I sat down and started to sob. My prayers were answered. Billy had found Jesus again. I ran up the stairs and showed my husband. It was the greatest gift.

My husband then called our pastor and asked if he would come over and bless our son before he left. He was at our house in less than half an hour.

There were at least five of us praying with our hands on my son. Oh, what a glorious feeling. Soon after that, his Staff Sargent was there to pick him up. Even though sadness took over my body, that glorious feeling remained with me.

The hurt I felt was unbelievable. It actually felt like a piece of my heart had been ripped right out of my chest. I did what every sane mother probably would have done the first day he left—I cleaned his room, touched, smelled, and remembered every piece of his clothing. I went into storage, took out a few baby clothes that I had saved, and cried over them. I washed up his little Christening outfit and white blanket and packed it up again.

Sharon couldn't understand why I was crying so much. She asked what I was going to do when she went away to college. I tried to explain to her that it just wasn't the same. She wasn't going to be leaving the country for four years, and I knew I would always have her. I guess she would have to wait to be a mother herself and know the feeling.

The next week was the toughest. I had already written my son a letter even though I didn't have an address to send it to. I had to wait for him to write to me first. It took exactly eleven days before we heard from him. I addressed my letter and sent it out. I did not miss a day without sending a letter, sometimes two. His first letter sounded really strange, and so official. At first, I thought they had brainwashed him already. My daughter said, "Wow, he writes really well kind of, too well." Then we opened up the second letter and we all got a laugh. It began, "What's up? They made us write the first letter."

Well, that was a relief. We kept receiving letters from him, all asking us to write. We couldn't understand why he wasn't getting any of our mail. He would write, "I hope it's because I'm so far away and the mail takes a long time, and not because you guys forgot me." Again, I would cry. We finally found out that the Marines hold the incoming mail for about two weeks so that the boys don't get homesick as fast. I guess that made sense. This was like a whole new life for him. All his letters were enthusiastic and filled with love. Could this really be the same boy? I wondered. Only one time did his letter sound a little depressing. He had said it was Sunday, and he was looking forward to going to church. He would have some peace and quiet where he could collect his thoughts. He said nobody would be screaming at him and nobody would be getting screamed at. That was the only down letter I received.

Meanwhile, Sharon was keeping us very busy. She was going to turn seventeen in April and it was time to look for a car for her. Since she had turned sixteen, she had said she wanted a fairly new Honda. That was asking pretty much since they were not cheap, but we were going to do our best to please her Then one day, she called me from her girlfriend's house and said she had found the car she wanted. I thought, oh, God, what could she be thinking? Where am I supposed to get the money from?

Then she explained the car to me. She thought it was an antique Cadillac or something. One thing she was sure of was that it was mint green. When I went to pick her up that night we stopped to look at it. It was a 1952 Packard, mint green. This was the car she wanted. Since we couldn't possibly keep up with the Jones' this was perfect.

She would be the safest kid driving, and we would be able to afford this car a lot easier than a Honda Accord. We did have to redo the interior and repaint the whole car. However, that was our business, so it was going to be a piece of cake. We only had less than two months to do all this in, and she let us know how many days we had left each and every day. As I said before, we worked best under pressure.

My daughter was once again the perfect child and back in the spotlight.

She and her brother became very close through their letters. Finally, all the hatred and jealousy were gone between them. She really missed her brother. She hadn't been working much since the mono, and she needed money for her new car. She had a brainstorm; "let's breed Shabi." "Lets", meaning, let mom do it. So there I was every night for two weeks at a breeder's house with little Shabi. Finally, they half-way consummated their date. The vet said we would have to wait and see what happens.

I got the bright idea of buying an at-home pregnancy test. Lord knows I know how to use them. The pharmacist said it would work with dogs, so I wasn't that off base. Anyway, I went outside with the dog and followed her around with a tiny, little cup. I took the test and waited two minutes. Guess what? It was negative. My daughter was very disappointed because now she had to get a real job. We still had six weeks before Billy would come home for leave and six weeks before Sharon turned seventeen.

The days seemed to drag when it came to my son, but they were moving too fast when it came to my daughter. I would write myself lists each week and see just how much I could accomplish. This was a little game that I played with my mind to keep myself busy.

I built my whole life around my son's letters. My husband would say if I didn't receive a letter within four days there was no living with me, but just one letter, even a small note, and I would be ecstatic—especially the Easter/Birthday card I got, which I carried all around with me to show all my friends at the diner. Every time I opened it, I cried. There was so much emotion between the two thin pages of that card.

Sharon's car was coming along well, I sanded the whole thing, and my husband repainted it. Mint green, of course. It came out beautiful. All we had to wait for now was the seat covers and the fabric for the interior. I ordered all of it from California.

Meanwhile, I had the vet over just to look at Shabi, as I was sure she was pregnant. She had put on about three pounds and she was beginning to fill up with milk. After a quick examination, the vet confirmed it was a false pregnancy. This really meant my daughter had to get a real job.

Over the past couple of months, we had thought our son had matured a great deal, and a letter my daughter received about two weeks prior to his leave only enforced our thoughts, beliefs, and wishes. The letter went something like this:

Dear Sharon,

What's up? It's Sunday now. I just got back from church. Nineteen days left. I can't wait. So how is everything? I'm coming to school with you one day when I get home, in uniform. I can't wait to come home and hang out with everyone. I was thinking about it and my friends are low-lifes. I mean, the are cool and all, but they are going to be doing the same shit five years from now, and I'll be all over the world making money, and probably have my own house, car, wife, and kids. I grew up in three months. From here on out I'm on my own. That is cool, though. I miss and love you.

Love, Billy

This is what we prayed for all along. As I read the letter over and over again, the words were embedded in my mind and in my heart.

The days were finally passing, and graduation was sneaking up on us, as was Sharon's birthday. Her parts still did not come in to finish her car, but she was going to have to live with it. It was now three days before we were to leave for Paris Island, South Carolina. I had my father and his wife, (my logical mom) over for her birthday. My son was able to phone home for the first time in three months. We were all able to say a few words. It was just great to hear his voice. My dad's face turned so red; his eyes were filled with joy. He was so proud of his grandson, as were we all.

After they left, I had my husband get me a large box which I lined with towels. You see, I was still sure Shabi was pregnant. She had me up all night. All she did was hide and dig in the carpet. The next day I phoned the vet. I had to leave a message on her machine. I just wanted to know how far they carried out a false pregnancy. Was it right down to contractions? The vet got back to me saying if she was having contractions, she was having puppies. Two hours later we had two beautiful puppies. So much for a false pregnancy. Even with the dogs, the females have the doctors bewildered.

The departure day was finally here. My mom came over to watch all the animals. Again, we all piled into the trusty van. This time there were five of us until we hit Delaware. Then there were six. The next ten hours went pretty fast. It was about eleven at night when we retired to our rooms at Beaufort Lodge. The kids went into one room and my husband and I went into another. It was really easy to go to sleep after that long ride.

Paris Island was beautiful. The grounds were immaculate.

Everything and everyone seemed to glow with perfection. There he was, out on the parade field practicing for graduation. We had to wait until they were given orders to leave the parade field. We now had five hours to catch up on three months. He looked so handsome. He seemed to have grown so much He stood so straight and with such authority and pride. We could not believe it. Before our eyes was the most precious gift one could ever ask for. We talked and laughed and cried I especially cried when he told me his orders were communication in the infantry—the one word I didn't want to hear. Why couldn't he do communications behind a desk? I knew I had to face reality.

This was the Marines. It was just that sick feeling I guess every mother feels when her son enters the armed forces. I guess crying at that time was my way of dealing with it.

The five hours seemed to have flown right by. It was time for us to once again retire at Beaufort Lodge. This time it was going to be a little more difficult to go to sleep. Tomorrow was the big day—graduation. We were all up at six AM for breakfast. All six of us hustled to get to the parade field early to get good seats, right smack in the front. It was sort of chilly, especially when the wind blew. But I wasn't shaking from chills. It was all nerves.

The emotions were spinning around inside of me like a cyclone.

There is no way to explain just how I felt. I guess proud would be the word right next to thankful. Everything went perfectly. Within two hours we were all in the van, this time seven of us, anxious to get back home. The ride had seemed never-ending. Once in Delaware, we dropped off one girl. Then the kids spread out a little more and went to sleep. The next hour and a half went pretty fast. We were home again with our son. This time he would stay with us for ten days, then he would be off to North Carolina. Each time it would get a little easier, though I was sure it would never be easy.

IN CLOSING, I THOUGHT

So what am I doing for myself these days? For one thing, I am finally writing this book. I also started a small business of my own. I make custom- covered photo albums and sell them at parties, similar to Tupperware parties. I knew I was good at something. I also joined the gym with my daughter. She encouraged me, not that I was fat or out of shape. She said it was to have fun. I didn't fall for that reason, but I decided to give it a shot. Now I have to buy some sweats.

As for my husband, he is doing well. We are getting along pretty well.

We are two people living together, working together, in each other's sight twenty-four hours a day, for the past twenty years. I guess we are doing something right, having to survive all those ups and downs. I guess you could say we are doing pretty darn good.

I am sure every parent has said to themselves, "Where have I screwed up?" Well, let me tell you, parents can only do so much. Don't listen to all those talk and radio shows where they bash the parents and say if there was discipline at home this wouldn't have happened. Either they don't have children of their own or they are just that children—not teenagers.

A parent can plant the seed, but where it grows from there is out of your control. I am not saying I was the perfect parent, but I did do all the right things. I taught them pre-education, manners, and all about the church and God. I raised two children at the same time, the exact same way, and look what I got. So don't let anyone say it is totally the parent's fault.

I think it is time to end my book. Not to short-change my daughter, but you see, she is the ideal child. Scratch that. She has already become someone very special. I don't foresee any major problems with her, thank God. And besides, if I continue this book, I do believe it would become very boring. There is no way I could top any of the events my son has put me through. You have to have faith in your child, faith in yourself, and most of all faith in God. There is no way we can do it by ourselves; we must remember to thank Him for all His little blessings.

These words came to me one night when I was in a deep sleep. I woke up trembling and wrote them down. I always have a pencil

and paper next to my bed just in case something like this happens. Anyway, this was the quote that I wrote down, I didn't understand it, but I was sure it would be of some importance:

"Don't listen

Because you won't understand us

Just think of us and we'll know you are there."

I can now sit back and absorb every word of it. It was my children speaking. Maybe it was all children speaking. We have to be there for them.

WHAT LIFE HANDS YOU

Originally when I wrote this book it only had 18 chapters, I gave a copy to Sharon my daughter when she turned twenty-one, because I felt she was mature enough to appreciate it. I waited until Billy, my son, was twenty-five to give him a copy, only because I knew any sooner, he would have taken offense. When he finished reading it, he told me he really didn't like it. He asked me why I didn't finish writing it. I told him I ended there because I wanted it to have a happy ending. He said, "Mom, life doesn't always have a happy ending." Unfortunately, he was right. So I dedicate the second half of this book to my beloved son, Billy Costello.

MAMAS, DON'T LET YOUR BABIES GROW UP TO BE MARINES.

I wish I could have ended my book here and now. It would be just the perfect ending, but such as life, I don't think there are perfect endings anymore.

It was now October 1997. My son was being shipped off to Okinawa. For a two-year term. As he left between the tears and the kisses, I prayed he would be safe. He wasn't even gone three days and I remember it took almost eighteen hours to get there, we got a call. Billy had been stopped at customs in the Japan Airport with some type of animal steroids in his belongings. All he could tell us was that he would probably get discharged from the marines.

We didn't hear from him for a few weeks. We figured they were trying to work something out since the steroids were legal in Japan, but they were not accepted by the marines. The laws were very different in Japan, the boys were no longer American citizens. They lost all their rights when they landed on that island.

Meanwhile, my daughter got her acceptance letter from N.Y.U. She was so excited, being the only student from our little town to go to N.Y.U. We were just wondering how much money the tree in the back yard was going to produce. Tuition for a year was $32,000.00 But this was what Sharon wanted so this was what Sharon was going to get.

Christmas was coming upon us fast. I had to get all my packages to mail to Japan. This was Billy's favorite holiday, and his first time away from home. So I had to make it as special as I could. I sent a Polaroid camera so he could send me back a picture of him. It had already been a couple of months since I had seen him, and I really missed him. He said because the laws were different in Japan they were still working on the steroid issue. He said he was still confined to the barracks, which I was happy about. At least, he wouldn't get in any trouble.

Christmas came and went. It just wasn't the same. The letters from Japan were really sweet. He would tell us that, next paycheck he would send some gifts home. We knew he spent his money as fast as he got it. But at least the thought was there. He meant well. Finally, I got a picture of him. He looked so big and strong and handsome.

That night I had this really weird dream. In my dream was this woman, whom I had never seen before, with her arms filled with folded uniforms and camouflage outfits. I was standing outside my house by the statue of the Virgin Mary, just admiring her. When this strange woman walked up to me and handed me all these uniforms. She said my son had left the Marines a few days ago. I was so upset because he hadn't got in touch with me. I woke up crying.

All day I couldn't get the dream out of my head. Then a funny thing happened. Some man came to our house and gave my husband a camouflage jacket and a vest. For what reason we don't know. We didn't even know the man.

That night I went down to the basement to ride my exercise bike. I had my son heavy on my mind, so I took his favorite book, "Sounder" off the shelf and decided to read it while I peddled. I had just turned to the fourth page when the phone rang. I picked it up at the same time Bill picked it up, upstairs. It was the lieutenant in Okinawa. He was in charge of my son's platoon. He called to inform us that Billy and another marine were in Japanese custody after being arrested for a fight outside a bar. As he talked my body felt like all the blood was being drained from it. The lieutenant tried to comfort us and said, "Let the marines handle it."

So for about three weeks, we did what he said. Our correspondence was only phone calls to the lieutenants which were in the middle of the night, because of the time difference. I happened to be watching CNN when I saw this lawyer talking about American prisoners in foreign countries and the abuse they received. I called CNN and they contacted the lawyer for me. He called me immediately and said the marines already had abandoned my son and the other boy. He also said that if we didn't go public, they may die there.

We went public and the press was very helpful or should I say interested. I was in touch with them every day with an update. I also sent a letter to President Clinton but received no response.

The letter:

April 26, 1998

President Clinton,

I previously sent you a copy of the letter enclosed on April 2, 1998. I am sure if this were your daughter or another family member you would have reacted in some manner. Both of these boys have been in a Japanese prison for over fifty days. The marines have completely abandoned them. They allowed the boys to be subjected to twenty-three days of interrogation without any representation. That is in violation of United States Law title 22 of sec. 1732. Lieutenant Colonel Craig F. Meyers upon our attorney's request was supposed to tell our boys to agree to bail, so they could be placed in the military brig, while our attorney could do some investigating. Instead, he advised William that it would not be wise to leave the Japanese jail and possibly lose time served. He also told him that his parents were blowing this all out of proportion. The boys were advised to plead guilty, pay all damages, and serve time. Once they were released from the Japanese prison, we were told, they were to be discharged from the Marines. I believe that would be a dishonorable discharge. Then they would be flown directly to California.

The Marines have already convicted them before any type of trial.

The boys acted in self-defense. Only the Americans were arrested.

The Japanese civilian sustained a fractured cheek bone. My son had a split lip which required stitches, but my son refused any medical attention.

Lieutenant Colonel Craig F. Meyers violated the boy's constitutional rights by telling them to stay in the Japanese prison. The marines are willing to sacrifice our boys to save face and not make waves with the Japanese. I am going to do everything in my power to make this known to the American public.

Cheryl Costello

(Speaking for the Costello and Stubbs families)

My husband got in touch with the Japanese attorney representing our son. He proceeded to say he was going to have the boys plead guilty and spend three years on the mainland in prison. My husband told him if he did that, that would be the last trial he would ever do. And furthermore, he would go there personally and kill him.

The next day that Japanese lawyer walked into the courtroom and removed himself from the case. The American attorney who had filled us in on everything found a Japanese lawyer my husband could talk to.

So, after many appearances in the newspapers, my husband was off to Japan for what was supposed to be a week. Meanwhile, I drove from New Jersey to Washington D.C., for a meeting with our congressman and senator. When I explained the whole situation, of which they were totally unaware, they cried with me. To think you're no longer an American, you have no rights, and the marines won't back you. Instead, they want you to say you're guilty when you're not, just to keep peace. Things were going to be different now, we now had the United States government backing us. Our senator sent a letter to the Prime Minister of Japan, stating that the two boys should be released, or severe actions would be taken.

My husband entered the base in Okinawa receiving the cold shoulder. He received very little help from the marines. The writer from the Stars and Stripes helped him find accommodation, translators, and guides. All of this would be very expensive, about $250.00 a day.

My husband finally got to visit my son. The guard called Billy's name and said he had a visitor. Billy figured it was another lawyer. When he looked up and saw his father he wept, as did my husband. Billy was at least thirty pounds less... I know because I got his picture the night before this whole mess happened. He was filthy with sores on his feet, his lip was torn but had already healed. He had the same clothes he had on six weeks ago.

Billy explained what he could to my husband about that night. It was the first day he was allowed off base. The boys were leaving the bar after a heavy night of drinking. He asked the civilian for a light. The civilian said, "Fuck you, American, go home." My son then said, "I hope you and your family get in an accident." The civilian then karate-chopped Billy between the eyes and broke his nose. Billy then hit the civilian once in the jaw, breaking it.

They were detained for three days before being put in a cell. They ate fish heads in soup and showered twice a week. Showers consisted of two buckets, one to wash with and one to rinse with, as they stood over a drain, while the guards stood around and gawked at them.

All Billy did was read the bible every day and never talked. That was all we ever heard happened. But I know in my heart much more happened because he was never the same.

While my husband was there, he raised all kinds of hell. He even told the judge that if he had been in Washington when we bombed Japan, he would have dropped twenty-two on them instead of two. In fact, that night my husband got a call from the senator saying to be careful. He couldn't protect him over there. My husband's stay was extended to almost two and a half months.

That's two and a half months of no salary coming in to pay our bills. I started cleaning houses during the day... between talking to the papers...the senator and the congressman. I spent nights on the phone with my husband. Our phone bill was about $1700.00 a month for about four months since the whole mess started.

Somehow my daughter and I managed. I bargained with all the bill collectors; we ate dented canned foods and I sold a litter of puppies.

Finally, my husband came home, Sharon graduated from high school with high honors and was president of the Student Council. None of this commotion affected her social life. She was so beautiful and so confident in herself.

When her father was gone, she got a job at Hooters, she was eighteen and there was no one telling her, "No."

The boys were going to court for sentencing on July 22, which was my husband's birthday. We both decided to go back to Japan to make sure the marines didn't play any stunts and that the boys did get justice. For the first time ever in Japan, both Americans received bail, and then both received a suspended sentence. The boys made history!

Billy spent the next two months in the Marine Brig on base. He was discharged and released to us.

THE HOME COMING

We had thousands of yellow ribbons tied on the trees in the front yard. We planned a large picnic for the next day. All our relatives, neighbors, the priests, and the police were coming. And all my son's and daughter's friends too. It had to be 95 degrees all day, the yard and pool were very busy. There was plenty of food and soda...no alcohol.

By nine o'clock all the adults had gone home. My husband and I went to bed totally exhausted and relieved. We had our son home again. We must have passed right out.

About two hours later my daughter's best friend was standing in our bedroom crying. She said the boys were going to fight. We ran downstairs to Billy's room to find that the tables were covered with bottles of liquor, every kind you could think of. My husband went crazy. Since we haven't had any alcohol in our house for over fifteen years. First Bill threw the glass table holding a lot of the liquor, then we separated the boys. Evidently, my daughter took the drink away from my son's friend who was drinking it out of a bowl like a dog. He got angry with her and hit her in the chest knocking her down.

We tried to pull the boy up the stairs so he could leave. He was twenty-one years old, about six feet, four, and extremely intoxicated. We got him up about four steps when he pulled us right down. My husband then picked up some of the broken glass and took it to the trash. When Bill came back down the stairs Billy's friend was lying on the floor next to the air conditioner. Billy had punched him once and he fell on the air conditioner, which broke his jaw.

This was one of Billy's best friends. He lived at our house every summer and would go on all our vacations with us. Anyway, he decided to press charges against Billy.

So once again the clouds were beginning to shadow over my son. We put the court off for about a year.

It was now September 1998 and Sharon was getting ready to move to New York, to go to N.Y.U. We bought everything a first-year student would need to go to a big university. We packed everything in the van and left for New York. Me, my husband, Billy, and my daughter's best friend, oh, and Sharon.

As we were unloading everything, all Billy kept saying was how lucky Sharon was to be going to such a nice school. All I could think was how sad I felt for him. We spent all our money on his lawyers and the rest on Sharon's school. He always seemed to get the shitty deal.

One thing seemed like a bright light; Billy was interested in Sharon's best friend. Their romance seemed to bloom. Sharon came home almost every weekend. She really was hating the city.

That was exciting to me. All I could think of was cutting the tuition bill in half. By December she was ready to come home. She enrolled herself into Monmouth University and would wind up getting a full tuition grant, because of her grades and we were pretty poor.

The first half of the year she spent in the dorm. Then, of course, they just had to rent a house. More room to party. She was still working at Hooters and paying some of her way.

THE SENTENCING

September came around again and that cloud was getting darker. We went to court with Billy for the fight in our basement. They took one look at my son's past and sentenced him to six months in jail. Again, they were taking my son away. I thought, "It was okay for that boy to hit my daughter in the chest, but it was wrong for a brother to defend his sister, in his own house."

So there we were, visiting our son behind bars again. His regular visitors were my husband and I, Billy's good friend, and my daughter's best friend who was now Billy's girlfriend. Sharon rarely visited him, which pissed me off since it was in her defense he was there. But no one ever said anything. We just let it go.

It was the day after Thanksgiving and my mom called. She said she was having a lot of pain and could I please meet her at the hospital. This time she really looked bad. After they had done the certain procedure, she had a heart attack. Even though she survived it, we knew she wasn't going to make it.

She had already signed a DNR. I sat with her every night in the hospital. I would tell her to just pray that God would take her to peace. She would try to pray. It went like this:

Hail Mary, had a little lamb then she would say, "that's not right", she actually thought after signing the DNR she could call the doctor in and just let them put her to sleep. She was ready to go. she begged me to get Dr. Kevorkian.

Christmas was coming and I was so depressed. Again, my son was going to miss his favorite holiday. My mom was going to die any day and I was exhausted. Well, finally the holidays passed, the Millennium came, and three days later mom died.

We had the funeral without my son. She was cremated and we spread her ashes at Freehold Raceway in the first turn, just as she asked.

Billy made plans with his girlfriend to move into his trailer with him when he got out. So on January 27, 2000, we got our son back once again. About one month later Billy and I went to a pet shop.

Billy really wanted this bull dog. He was the cutest thing I ever saw. I would have to co-sign and the dog cost $2700.00. I myself am a very frugal person and this was way too much for me. Then the lady showed us the Pedigree papers and it just so happened that he was born on January 3, 2000. I couldn't risk the chance just maybe it was my mom. So I co-signed, and Billy named him Cerberus in Greek mythology, which means the three-headed dog that guards the gate to hell. Leave it to my son to give him that name.

It was a rough time for Billy and his girlfriend. She was a real prima donna. Don't get me wrong, he loved doing things for her. He loved her. She wasn't ready to get tied down, she wanted more than a trailer. She didn't fully leave the picture for another year. She just faded in and out, always leaving on worse terms than the time before.

Tattoos became the love of my son's life. Every month it was another. They were beautiful. He would always get the whole area filled in around the tattoo, so it looked like a tapestry.

My daughter had just finished a year and a half at Monmouth University and went on spring break to Panama City. That was when she and her roommates went to Panama City. After going to Florida and really seeing the party life, they couldn't get enough. So they all transferred to the University of West Florida. All including her best friend, my son's ex-girlfriend.

So we drove down to Florida, my daughter and me. It was twenty-one hours of pure talk. Not really a Kodak moment. She could hardly remember any of her childhood. All the stuff I busted my butt over to make her happy. There were certain parties and play dates that no longer existed in her memory. I pushed myself to play outside with them like soccer or in the snow. She seemed to have had more angry memories than good ones. No matter how much I tried to reminiscence, she had no recollection. All my efforts of trying to be the best mom just took a dive. Anyway, we made the best of our drive. So maybe Florida would be good for her. I tried to call home several times but didn't get an answer. I thought maybe the guys were having fun without us.

We were the first to get to the apartment, so we had to get everything set up. That was fun and so was shopping and spending that quality time with my daughter. I only hope she will remember.

After three days I flew home. That was when I found out why the guys didn't answer the phone. Poor Bacon, Sharon's pig had died, but not a quick death. My son had laid for hours in the barn as the poor pig squealed. Billy really had a big heart.

Billy was getting tired of living in the trailer. So he moved into a one- bedroom apartment. He set it up so cute. Ever since he became a marine he has been as neat as a pin. Everything must be in order and in its place. He was a perfectionist. Cerberus had to live with us because it was a garage apartment and he really couldn't do all those stairs. It didn't matter because Billy was working for my husband, so he was with the dog every day anyway.

Billy lived there for about six months when both my husband and I noticed he was becoming very depressed. We talked him into moving back home into the basement, which was finished like an apartment anyway. This lifted his spirits and brought a smile back to his face. A smile that had been gone for some time now. He was beginning to feel like he belonged somewhere. He went shopping and bought all the new furniture. The bedroom set was black lacquer with mirrors. The living room set was a leather sectional with two recliners and a pull-out bed. He made a real bachelor pad down there. He was eating meals with us and really being part of the family. It felt good to have him home and smiling again. Also to celebrate he had to get another tattoo or maybe two.

THE END OF COLLEGE BEING

FUN... REALITY SETS IN

It was July 2001. The fourth had just passed and I was so happy that neither of my kids was driving on the road during the holiday. On the night of the sixth, I had a really bad dream. I told my husband about it in the morning.

I dreamt I was driving with Sharon and we were involved in this huge accident. We both got up and walked away from it, but there were bodies everywhere. I felt better telling my husband hoping that would erase all the bad feelings I had inside.

Later that morning I left to go clean someone's house, when I got home Bill told me that Sharon had called with some bad news. Around two AM that morning she was driving her deadbeat of a boyfriend home from work when a drunk driver hit her head on and drove right over the roof of her car. By some miracle, she survived it, even though she did have some major injuries.

Her friend was okay too. Somehow my dreams always warn me about my family, or maybe they just prepare me so that I can handle whatever life deals me. This would be the miserable start to Sharon's last year of college.

Somewhere along the way Sharon had bought a Chihuahua and named him Chico. He was by her side every moment of the day, actually he was in her pocketbook.

Sharon came home for Christmas, and we had our whole family together even though there were only four of us and the grandparents, it still felt good.

Then Sharon's boyfriend flew in to meet all of us. He was nothing like the boys she dated all through high school. He was a hippy, who really didn't take care of himself. But because he was Sharon's friend we welcomed him into our home.

February came along with some of the worst news you can imagine.

Sharon's first boyfriend had hung himself. When Sharon got the news she was devastated. I thought she was going to have a nervous breakdown. We flew her in for the funeral. She couldn't talk; I never saw her so bad. There was nothing I could say or do to make her heart stop hurting. I don't think she said more than ten words during the three days she was home. She flew back to Florida with hundreds of pictures so she could keep the memories fresh in her heart.

She had only about three and a half months left before she would graduate and maybe come home. I really didn't think she ever wanted to come back home. She was still dating the boy we met at Christmas. Besides being filthy I was sure he was mentally unstable too. He was babysitting or should I say dog sitting for Sharon while she was at work. Chico really didn't care for the boy either. He would always try to nip him or growl at him. I always felt animals are the best judge of people. Anyway, this mental boyfriend must have hit this five-pound Chihuahua against the wall and killed it. He then buried it before calling Sharon to tell her he was dead. Sharon called me hysterical screaming, "Chico is dead!" All I could tell her was to stay away from that boy, he was evil. That was the first time I ever told her who to date. Then we flew her home again for another weekend.

Through all those distractions she was able to stay on the honor roll and graduate. She had attended three colleges and was still able to graduate within four years with a bachelor's degree in criminal justice. Although that degree would never be put to use, it was a great accomplishment.

Graduation time was here. Billy flew down to Florida with about seven of his friends. They rented a huge beach house and partied every night. Bill and I flew down the day before. Sharon was late getting to graduation, which was to our benefit. There were about two thousand graduating and we would have never been able to find her. So when she walked in late, we saw where she sat. All the boys were in the balcony drunk and hung over. Sharon was so excited to have her brother and friends rooting for her. Afterward, we all went back to the beach house to have a barbeque. Everything seemed to work out perfectly. Also, Sharon had purchased a new puppy. He was almost a Chihuahua, and she named him Mikko.

For Sharon's graduation, she took me on a cruise to Mexico. While driving to the ship which took about seven hours, she told me something that was special. She told me that she believed Chico died for her. That was the only way he could save her from that mental boyfriend. She said she wasn't sad about Chico dying, she was thankful. Our trip was the greatest. After the cruise, I flew back home. Sharon didn't have any intentions of moving back. She enjoyed her life in Florida.

Billy liked the idea of living in the beach house with a couple of friends. So in the fall about four of them got together to share a winter rental here on the Jersey shore. He was having a blast and visiting us on weekends. Billy really enjoyed being around a lot of friends all the time. He hated spending time alone. Bill and I were enjoying the privacy for the first time. We seemed to worry a little less. Both of our kids seemed to be a little more responsible.

Although Sharon was only waitressing and tending bar she was still pulling most of her weight.

ONE INSANE SUMMER

It was May 2002. Bill and I were celebrating our Twenty-Sixth wedding anniversary. Billy had to move back home because the winter rental was over. It was a little hard getting used to having someone else in the house all the time again. We built a beautiful deck on the back of our house for our anniversary.

I called it our retirement deck.

Billy was in the tattoo parlor, getting another tattoo when a flashy blonde from New York walked in. For him, it was love at first sight. He was twenty- five and she was thirty. It was so much fun listening to him tell us about her.

His eyes would just twinkle. He couldn't wait to bring her home to meet us.

She was about five feet tall and a very revealing dresser. She had been divorced and owned her own home in New York. I wondered why she would be interested in my son, who was just starting out in life. She had very expensive taste and tried very hard to look a lot younger. Billy was tall, big, and handsome, and she did look good being escorted by him to all the fancy restaurants. He maxed out both his credit cards and any money he had saved.

He followed her around like a puppy. At first, I thought maybe an older woman would be good for him but soon I would be seeing her in a much different way.

They had been together for almost three months and Billy still seemed happy. She had gotten tickets to see Bon Jovi, but she had already asked her girlfriend to go. So she had Billy make reservations at the big hotel and told him to wait there for her until after the concert. Well, he waited about six hours at the bar. He was totally intoxicated when she called from the car on the way back from the concert. She must have had a man with her because Billy could hear him.

That blew the fuse in Billy's head. He went crazy, he broke mirrors, lights, and walls in the hotel. He ran out to the parking lot just as they were pulling up. He pulled his girlfriend out of the car by her hair and slammed her against the car, causing her purse to empty in the parking lot. He then jumped in his GMC and sped off. The hotel had called the police and while the police were getting the report from his girlfriend, they heard about an accident involving a GMC on the bridge.

All Billy remembered was the police coming up to his car. Billy called us around eight AM from the police station. He said he had been arrested and we had to come and bail him out. He was in the Bergen County police station. When we got there and saw Billy our mouths dropped. All he had on were his boxers and socks. He had two black eyes, lumps all over his head including the back of his head. He had bruises on his chest and paddle marks, the kind the first-aid would use. He also still had the little stickers that connected to a heart monitor. He had no ID bracelet from the hospital.

We asked the police what happened. They said he destroyed the hotel; beat up his girlfriend and got into an accident on the bridge. We asked what happened to him. They said it happened in the accident and he was taken to Jersey City Medical Center. The police officer also said they took blood and Billy was going to be charged with a DUI. We bailed him out and took him home. At first, I was real angry at him for even touching his girlfriend. I thought he had learned something from the fight his father and I had years before. But the more I looked at him the sorrier I felt for him.

We had his truck towed home. There was only about three hundred and fifty dollars' worth of damage. There was no blood in the truck and Billy was covered with blood when we picked him up. So Bill and I began to do a little investigating. We went to the hospital where Billy was taken. After about an hour of searching for his file, they said we must have the wrong hospital. My husband gave his business card to the gentleman who was trying to be helpful and said if he found any information to please call us. It was exactly one week later he called us. He said Billy was brought into the hospital as John Doe. The only paper that had Billy's name on it was blood work for the police. Billy didn't remember ever going to a hospital. He must have been knocked unconscious. He did remember somebody kneeling on his chest but nothing else.

Again, we would have to go to court for our son. The girl didn't press any charges, instead, she asked for money for her camera and cell phone.

Thirteen hundred dollars to be exact. Billy received one-year probation, anger management classes, which cost eight hundred dollars, classes with a motor vehicle, which cost six hundred and fifty dollars, drug counseling, which was free, loss of his license for two years, and 180 hours of community service. We could not prove that the officers beat Billy because there were no witnesses.

So summer was over, Billy's ex-girlfriend was going back to New York and didn't need her boy-toy anymore. Billy had to file for bankruptcy because she had drained him dry. This was one lesson he would never forget. To this day, we have never been billed from the hospital.

A FRESH START

It was now January 2004, a new year, a new beginning. Billy started his community service. He was the one to sort the bottles at the township dumps. He really didn't mind going, he always had fun with whomever he was with.

He always brought home paperback books he found to read. You would have thought he found gold at the dumps. His probation officer was a jerk, he would always push Billy's buttons to see how angry he would get. Thank God, Billy kept his temper most of the time. Anger management classes were a joke. He would always say how pissed off he was when he had to go, which was every Thursday night. Motor vehicle school was every other Monday night. So I was his chauffeur and his support. I was always there when he was feeling down, which was pretty often.

On a happy note, Sharon had a new boyfriend for about a year and a half now. We were really happy with him. He was kind, considerate, and loved animals. He was also clean-cut. This was a miracle that she was able to find someone who was so perfect for her. They bought a house in North Carolina last summer. We were just waiting for him to pop the question. We knew it would be sooner or later, hopefully sooner.

Billy was becoming a hermit in his room in the basement. Since he didn't have a license, he hardly went out. He really missed being with his friends. All he did was work, go to classes for driving and anger, and report to his probation officer. The only thing he really enjoyed was getting tattoos.

His body was pretty much covered, but he always thought he needed more. We became very close. He would talk to me about everything. He always felt his life was going nowhere. Even though he made $42.00 an hour, he never had any money. Most of it went to pay his fines and surcharges. If he had any left, he would take it to a nearby bar and treat all his friends. By the beginning of the week, he would be broke again. He talked to me about girls and said there wasn't any one that was right for him. Don't get me wrong, he dated many girls but since he was hurt by the last two, he didn't think he would get serious any time soon. He was very depressed and often talked about death. I asked him if he was thinking about suicide and he answered very angrily saying, "No! That's the coward's way out!" He felt there should be something more to life than just this.

Billy was getting ready to celebrate his twenty-sixth birthday on May 12. He was really planning it right. He rented a bus and a driver to take him and about fifteen of his friends to the shore. Since he didn't have a license and he didn't want any of his friends to get a DUI, the bus would pick them up at our house at six o'clock and bring them all back at about two AM.

First, they all go to the Japanese restaurant for sushi and from there walk to the closest bar. Everything was going as planned. They all ate and were drinking pretty heavily. A fight broke out. Now the story goes like this; they were all outside the bar and some of Billy's friends were fighting with some other guys.

Billy was trying to pull some guys apart, and the police grabbed him. Billy is always the first one the police grab. I think it's because of his appearance.

He's tall, really built, his head was shaved bald, and he had his shirt off so they could see his entire body was tattooed and pierced. He looked like he was in trouble. Billy's friend pleaded with the officer to let Billy go. He said if you take him then take me too. So both of them were locked up for the night. The bus dropped everyone else off at the house.

Billy and his friend each received a summons for disorderly persons and a twelve hundred dollar fine.

Billy never mentioned the arrest to his probation officer, otherwise he would have been charged with violating his probation.

It was midnight, June twenty-fifth when the phone woke us. Sharon crying hysterically. Bill couldn't understand a word she was saying so he handed me the phone. These were tears of joy! Finally, her boyfriend asked her to marry him. That kind of pone call in the middle of the night is good. We were so excited! Billy had heard the phone downstairs and came running into our room. He thought something might be wrong. He was very happy about his sister's good news. But I could tell deep inside he was a little jealous that she was getting her life together. First a house and now she was getting married.

She did ask him to be at her wedding party, which made him feel included and maybe a little special.

Bill and I made a trip to North Carolina two weeks later to give our congratulations and to help start making plans for the wedding. I planned an engagement party combined with a twenty-year sobriety party for my husband. This way we could kill two birds with one stone. I invited about seventy people for a barbeque and pool party. The tents were set up the night before. Bill and I had worked in the yard for two months to make everything perfect.

The future in-laws were flying up from Florida. We had people coming from Pennsylvania and New York. This was going to be a great party! The invitations stated that the party would begin at two o'clock. Well, at exactly two o'clock the heavens opened up and it rained on our parade. The rain never stopped. So I had seventy people and ten dogs, nine were mine and one was Sharon's in my little six-room house.

Billy was the greatest. He greeted people at their cars and walked them in with an umbrella. He ran outside to the coolers to get them drinks, still cooked on the grill in the rain. He loved being around a lot of people. That was when his smile would shine the most. Everyone complimented me on what a fine young man I raised. Yes, I was very proud of him. The party was great, no one seemed to mind being inside. No one except me. All I could think about was how hard I worked to make my yard look so pretty and nobody was able to see it.

THE FIRST FUNERAL

The fall was here again. This meant we had to cover up the pool and pack all the yard furniture away. It was much easier this year because we had Billy to help us. Unfortunately for him, he was laid off for the winter. He was able to get a few side jobs a couple of days a week. The other days he would spend time at home in the kitchen. He loved to cook and he loved to eat. He would prepare all our dinners and desserts. He just didn't like to do the dishes, so that was my job. I was fine with that because I loved to clean. He was even helping with the laundry, especially since he was so particular with the way he liked his stuff done. It was really fun having him around the house. We were still making our trips to anger management, counseling, and reporting.

And he was still able to make payments on his fines with his unemployment checks.

It was eight PM on November 3 when we got a call from the nursing home. Bill's mom was not doing well and they felt we should be there. So Bill and I went to the nursing home to meet with about eleven other members of his family. We all sat around her bed and watched her sleep. Everyone was talking and reminiscing about all the good times. She was sleeping so peacefully, then she took a slight sigh. And that was that. Mom went ever so peacefully to the other side. I was glad my husband was there to witness it and know she had no pain. We knew she was in a much better place. I called Sharon and she and her Fiancé were to fly in the next day. That night when we returned home we told Billy. We were hoping there wouldn't be any argument about him attending the funeral. There wasn't. He knew out of respect for his father and his grandmother he would be there. Bill's sisters made all the preparations for the funeral. I was amazed at how well he was handling everything.

Two days had passed, and it was time to go to the funeral home. Billy had his father tie his tie, and so did Sharon's Fiancé. We tried to prepare Billy for what was going to be. We all walked into the main entrance of the funeral home. There were people standing everywhere. Some were looking at pictures, some were chatting in groups, and some were weeping and paying respects to mom. Billy just stood there taking it all in. Then he walked up to the casket with us, knelt down, and said a prayer. Trying not to let the tears run down his face, he still had to be a tough guy. Then he went to the back of the room where everybody was chatting and stood with his sister. He said, "Sharon is this what a funeral is like?" She replied, "Yes." He then asked her, "Please Sharon, when I die, promise me you'll have a keg of beer and a pig roast". He didn't want everybody just standing around crying. He wanted them to have a big party. After the funeral, he must have told at least six of his friends what he thought about funerals and what he wanted.

Two weeks later my uncle died. So, without even having to ask Billy, he came to the funeral. Can you imagine! Two funerals in two weeks. All my relatives complimented him on how handsome he was in a suit. They said at the barbecue he was pretty scary in just shorts and all those tattoos.

Finally, November was over. That was a sad month. We were now getting ready for Christmas. I put the tree up early to pick everyone's spirits up in the house. Billy really loved Christmas. He had a list of all the things he had to buy everybody. Of course, I had to order the stuff or go shopping for it since he didn't drive. He ordered a creeper for his father to use in the shop. I took him to the mall, and he also bought his father the CD by Tim McGraw, 'Live Like You Were Dying'. For Sharon and her Fiancé, he bought a game and a tool set in a pink case. He also wanted to get them a stool for the bathroom as a joke because they were both so short. Mine would be a surprise. I would have to wait for Christmas.

Billy had finally finished his 180 hours of community service. He finished all his anger management and motor vehicle classes. And he was done with counseling. This was also his last visit to his probation officer. Billy was so proud of himself, and so were we. I dropped him off at probation for the last time. Then I ran to do a few last-minute errands. I was waiting in the parking lot for Billy expecting to see his bright smile when he came out frowning. I asked what the problem was. It seems he was finished with probation, but his probation officer was going to violate him for being arrested in May on his birthday. So, Billy now had to wait for another court date to come in the mail.

Our attorney thought that the probation officer might have been messing with Billy's head and told us not to worry, just to wait it out.

Poor Billy, it just seemed like every time he took a step forward, he took two steps backward. He was trying so hard to get his life back on track. He even made amends and bought the guy a drink that hit his sister and had him sent to jail for six months. He didn't want any more enemies. I decided this was a good time to do my powerful novena. I started it on December 17th and would end it on December 25th, Christmas Day. I was determined to help my son with his life. I prayed and I begged Baby Jesus to help Billy find peace and happiness in his life. I begged Him to let Billy love the Lord and Jesus and himself again. All I wanted was for Billy to be happy again. I said that prayer every day for nine days and I cried each time I said it.

It was now Christmas Eve and Bill and I were getting ready to go to mass. I asked Billy if he wanted to join us, but he said he didn't think so. I already knew what his answer would be, but I gave it a shot anyway. Bill said, "I'll light a candle for you and Sharon".

When we entered the church, I told Bill there probably wouldn't be any candles left to light. To my surprise, I was wrong. So Bill lit the candles and we both prayed. When it came time to receive communion I did as I've done for years. Since both the kids were about fourteen and decided, they didn't have to go to mass anymore, I received for them. I asked the Lord to bless them both while I have the host in my mouth.

We returned home from church to find Billy and an old friend from the school he went to for only six months, sharing a bottle of Jose Cuervo. Billy said a guy from work brought it over as a peace offering. He was happy there were no more bad words between them. Billy was going back to his friend's house for the night but promised to be home by seven. At seven o'clock I heard the front door squeak and again I was thankful. He was home safe.

Christmas day was here. Only my dad and his wife would be here with us to open gifts. Sharon and her Fiancé weren't coming until about the fourteenth of January. They were spending Christmas in Florida with his family. Billy was just like a little boy. He was so excited about everything. We bought him that memory mattress pad and pillows which he couldn't wait to try out. He also got a speed bag and a lot of clothes. Bill was really happy with his gifts, especially the country western tape from Billy. I got a diamond necklace from Bill and Billy gave me this beautiful cut crystal statue of a boy and girl kissing. It spins around with a light underneath it. He said he thought I would like the one kissing best, and that was why he picked that one. He was right, I loved it. We were all done with opening gifts. Billy made breakfast for all of us. He was tired since he had come in at seven AM. Anyway, he wanted a good reason to go downstairs and try out his new mattress.

Billy went to sleep for a couple of hours, and so did Bill and me. We all seemed to wake up at the same time, around six o'clock. We had lasagna for dinner. I wanted to soak in the tub and Billy wanted to get a shower before he went out with his friends. He had to wait until I filled the tub. Meanwhile, he groomed his beard in his bathroom. As always, he would call me in and ask, "Is it even on both sides, Mom?"

I would always say take a little off here just so he knew I was really paying attention. Finally, my bath was full. So I yelled to him that it was okay to shower. He was done in ten minutes. His friends came to pick him up while he was still getting ready. Bill let them in.

I was soaking in the bath, just relaxing. I could hear all their conversation. They were unwrapping the gifts Billy bought them. There was a lot of laughter. Then they got their coats and were leaving. Billy said goodbye to his father who was watching television in the bedroom. Then he started out the door and yelled, "See you later Mom."

I said, "Have fun". Usually, I say be careful but I knew he wasn't driving so I said have fun.

4:12 AM

Christmas was over as far as we were concerned. Bill and I retired early and watched a movie on cable. We watched "Meet the Parents". We both loved a good laugh. I know I fell asleep pretty early and I'm sure Bill soon followed me.

We were both sound asleep when we heard the doorbell ring. It was 4:12 AM. We both took notice of the time because Sharon's birthday is April 12. 4:12.

Bill looked out the bedroom window, the outside light was left on even though we knew Billy was staying at his friend's house for the night. Bill said, "Oh, no, it's two cops." I grabbed my robe and ran around the house trying to block the dogs from going to the front door. Remember we had nine dogs, so I was going crazy. All I could think was Billy got locked up again. I knew he couldn't have gotten into an accident because he wasn't driving.

When I came back into the hallway by the front door, Bill was standing there with both of his hands holding his head screaming, "No-no!" I felt my face begin to twist and asked, "Is he dead?" My body began to collapse. Bill caught me and held me so tight. We were both trembling all over. I was screaming, "Oh my God, my son is dead!" repeatedly. I'm not sure how long we were in the hallway, we could not seem to move. The police officers stayed right there with us. Finally, we made it to the kitchen. Somewhere we found the words to ask what had happened. They were our local police, so they had to call Point Pleasant Police station where the accident happened. Apparently, the Point Pleasant police told the officer that our son Billy and his friend had jumped from a moving vehicle. Billy's friend was in the hospital and Billy was killed instantly. The officers would not leave until we had someone come over to stay with us in our home.

We called a close friend of the family, who was also our retired police captain. Then we had to call to notify our daughter. I dialed her future mother-in-law's number in Florida. Sharon was still sleeping as was the rest of the family. I heard her mother-in-law -to-be say hello. And somehow I was able to get the words out, "Billy was killed tonight." Then Bill had to take the phone and ask her to give Sharon the news. Minutes later Sharon called back screaming, "No, this can't be true!" She wouldn't believe it. Thank God they had access to some mediation for her. Now they had to make all the arrangements to get her up here. Christmas is the busiest travel time of the year.

Bill began calling family members and I was calling some of Billy's friends. There was one thing that I kept repeating out loud. "The novena, I said the novena for nine days, praying that Billy would find peace and happiness, that he would love the Lord, Jesus and himself again. I ended that novena yesterday and today he is dead." I didn't want the Lord to take him. I wanted Billy to find peace here on earth and now he was gone. Was this my fault?

Did I rush his time here on earth? We also called the Pastor of our church.

One of the other priests came to our house first. He was very compassionate and told me that was the best prayer I could have made for Billy and not to feel one bit guilty. I tried not to, but in the back of my head, I still felt guilt. My heart just ached so terribly.

It was now about 7 a.m. and word had spread like wildfire. My house was full of family and friends. Everyone but my daughter. I really needed her there. I had to hold on to whatever I had left.

Sharon had called and said all the air arrangements were made and she would be here as soon as she could. The local restaurant had already sent over enough food for forty people. I was so glad everyone had taken over my house because I couldn't do a thing. Actually, I'm lying. I went into the laundry room where Billy had left his pile on the floor before he left. I did his laundry just the way he liked it done. Then I folded it and left it where I always do for him to put away. I knew he wasn't going to, but I felt it was what I had to do at the time.

It was now about ten AM and Billy's best friend came to the house. My husband asked him to go to the hospital to check on Billy's friend and to find out what exactly happened. I then had to go into Billy's room for the first time to pick out his final outfit. My sister-in-law and nephew came down to help me. It was so hard to open that door knowing he was never going to be in that room again. I could still smell him everywhere. I showed them where his new suit was and exactly what shirt and tie he had to wear with it. We grabbed his underwear, socks, and shoes, and we were out of there. Now we had to go to the funeral home to make all the arrangements. We asked Bill's other sister to accompany us and assist us. My brother and his wife met us there also. This was so difficult to accept. We were picking out a coffin and little cards. We were giving all this personal information about my son to a comforting stranger to finalize his last days on earth. The funeral would not be for another two days.

We returned home to find even more people in our house. Everything was a big blur. There was a lot of talking and reminiscing, but mostly a lot of tears. Billy's best friend returned with some disturbing news. As it turned out, only Billy had jumped from the car. Somewhere along the way, the story had gotten mixed up. The boys must have been talking during dinner about doing something drastic or extreme so they would have something to really talk about at the friend's wedding in April, which Billy was supposed to be in.

They were both extremely drunk when they left the restaurant, so his friend's girlfriend was doing the driving. She said Billy was very boisterous and kept opening the back door, saying he was going to jump. And then he did. His friend was passed out in the front passenger seat of the car. It was very hard to absorb all of this or even understand it. We knew Billy and the type of person he was. He lived life to the fullest and had very little fear. There was no one to blame or be angry with. It was something we would somehow learn to accept.

It was now beginning to get dark out and my heart was longing to hug my daughter. I knew she was going through hell trying to get home to us. Her plane had been delayed several hours, and she was calling every half hour. Our friends had offered to pick them up at the airport, it was obvious Bill or I could not drive. Finally, around eight-thirty my daughter walked through the front door. We all hugged and sobbed Sharon, Bill, and I. We didn't want to let go. She just kept saying, "How could this have happened?" There we stood in the same hallway, just as we did at 4:12 AM that morning. Still, not being able to believe any of this was real. I kept thinking it was a bad dream, and that I would wake up soon. We were all so drained and people just kept hugging each other and weeping for us.

We told Sharon about the arrangements we had made with the funeral home and that we were having Billy's body cremated. Billy always said he didn't want to be put in the dirt. I had ordered flowers from the family but we had put it in the newspaper announcement, in lieu of flowers, to please donate to the St. Jude's Children's hospital in Billy's name.

Just prior to Christmas I had made photo albums for both of the children, so ironically we had an entire box of all Billy's pictures in the living room.

Sharon and her best friend began picking out their favorite ones to be displayed at the funeral home. There were so many that they could not limit their choice to just a few. So they made a stack of about fifty, not including the large portraits. Sharon found the very best one of Billy laughing and was going to have copies made to give out at the viewing.

It was probably around midnight when all the company left. Bill, Sharon, and her Fiancé had retired for the night. I did not sleep that night. I was afraid to close my eyes. So when everyone finally did fall asleep, I got up. I had to take down the Christmas tree and all those decorations. This was not what Christmas was all about. This was Billy's favorite holiday and now I hated it. I didn't ever want to see another tree or Santa. I ripped down every decoration I could find. I was finished and my house looked like any other normal day.

That was what I was trying to find, normalcy.

That lasted for only a short while, then the doorbell rang. It was about seven AM. The girl who took care of our horses stopped by with enough coffee and donuts for about twenty-five people. Within a matter of an hour, my house was full again. Surprisingly all the dogs behaved so well. I guess they could sense something was wrong too. We were going to get a private viewing around 2 PM. We would have to wait that long because the hospital had kept his body until late the night before. It seems they had to do an autopsy. It would only be after the funeral that I would find that out. My husband knew I really didn't want them to cut my son open, but it seems it was the law. I felt they could have just done his blood alcohol level and saw that his head was split open to have known what had killed him.

Sharon and her friends kept themselves very busy making copies of Billy's picture. Four hundred to be exact. She also made a CD that would be played during the viewing. The first song on the CD would be, "Live Like You Were Dying", by Tim McGraw. Isn't that strange how things just seem to fall into place as if they were meant to be?

THE VIEWING

It was now two PM on the twenty-seventh of December. Again, we walked in through the back entrance of the funeral home. There were six of us. My dad, my stepmother, Sharon, her Fiancé, Bill and myself. Bill was holding me very tight. I felt as though I had no spine to hold me up. Bill and I would be the first allowed to view the body of our son. We walked through the doorway as if we were one person. This was the first time I was going to see my son and I wasn't sure what to expect. We walked over to the casket and there he lay. He looked so beautiful. He looked as if he were sleeping.

There wasn't a mark visible on him. He had a smile on his face, actually, it was more like a smirk. I practically climbed into the casket; it was all starting to set in. This was my son and here he was dead.

Then the rest of the family came in. Poor Sharon looked so weak and frail. Her fiancé stayed close by her side. She too tried to climb in and hug her brother. We only stayed about twenty minutes and then we had to leave him and go back to our very busy house.

By this time Sharon and I were on some heavy-duty drugs. I felt like I was in the ocean and I was just moving with the waves. I saw faces but couldn't hear a word they were saying. Later that night two women came from the church to make all the arrangements for the funeral. Sharon wanted the Prodigal Son to be read at the mass. She would also write some special words for her brother that her best friend would read for her. I'm glad she was there to talk to the women because words just couldn't leave my mouth.

Soon everyone left my house again. I was exhausted and fell asleep as soon as my head hit the pillow. I began to dream. First, I saw Billy as a baby crying and I couldn't get to him. Then all I could see was many faces crowding in my house. I began to scream and thrash my arms around. When I opened my eyes, I felt Bill embracing me with all his might. He was my backbone.

He gave me another pill and watched me sleep the rest of the night. I can't tell you which day was the hardest. Each day was more difficult in its own way. I woke up early and began cleaning. I had to make sure my house was in some kind of order. Again, another friend came by with coffee and donuts. I made sure Bill's suit was pressed and ready.

We left the house around one thirty PM. The funeral home was only a few minutes from us. The back of the car was full of portrait-size pictures and a box of photos. This time we would enter the funeral home by the front door. The pictures were put in place. There were flowers from wall to wall. And right there in the middle of everything was my son. Blessing number one. He looked so handsome and peaceful. Again I hugged and kissed him. My tears began to spot his suit. I touched his face and beard and told him that both sides were even. Because that would have been what he would have asked me. I put an instant camera and a picture of Cerberus, his bulldog, in the casket. He loved taking candid pictures of everybody, so I wanted him to take some pictures as soon as he got to heaven. Once I was by his side I never left. Bill stood behind me to hold me up when I became weak. Sharon had her Fiancé as her pillar.

At first most of the people there were family but then the room began to fill. All of Billy's friends, one by one approached us. Each one would help me sob a little bit more. Each one would bring a different memory to my mind.

When I hugged them it felt like I was hugging a piece of Billy. Sometimes I didn't want to let go. I would whisper in their ear, "Please don't do this to your mother." And when their parents came to pay their respects, I would whisper to them, "Don't let the little things bother you, life is too short."

Finally, around four thirty, the place was almost empty. Only the immediate family was still there. We all kissed Billy and told him we would be back.

We had less than two hours before we would have to return. So again we squeezed into my house. I swear the house was getting smaller. There were so many people and so much food.

People traveled from New York, Pennsylvania, North Carolina, Virginia and Florida. Everyone was much more somber, not much chit-chat was going on. So many people tried to get me to eat, but food was the farthest thing from my mind. I was surviving on hot tea. We decided to leave a little earlier and get to the funeral home by six thirty.

Much to our surprise, the parking lot was nearly full and the funeral home was already packed with people. The director said he opened the doors early because a line was beginning to form. I rushed over to be by Billy's side gripping Sharon's hand so tightly. Within minutes the line was out the door and began to wrap around the building. Again, one by one family and friends began to pay their respects. As before, Bill stood behind me and physically supported me. We thought the afternoon viewing was tough; we were not ready for this. Hundreds of people waited in line for almost three hours. So many beautiful girls came up to the casket sobbing while they hugged and kissed me, they would tell me how much they loved Billy. All this time I thought he couldn't get a girlfriend. He just never found the right one.

It was now around nine thirty and our pastor asked everyone to bow their heads and pray for Billy. Then he began to speak of how depression affects certain people in certain ways, especially around the holidays. I could feel my face begin to twitch, my whole body felt like it was being suffocated. When he finished, my husband stood up and said, "Father, Billy did not commit suicide, he just did a stupid stunt." The pastor just said, "Oh really?" I couldn't believe that he just assumed that Billy had committed suicide. After that, some of Billy's close friends, around twenty of them, went up to the casket. They made a half circle around it and formed a huddle. They all banded together, hung their heads, and with many tears they prayed. They remained there for over fifteen minutes. I could not believe how many lives Billy had touched in his short life. He always wanted to be surrounded by friends. Everybody loved him.

THE FUNERAL

I woke up begging God to give me the strength to get through today.

My husband had been a rock through all of it. I think he felt he had to be strong for me. He was right. I don't think I would have gotten through it without him. Again, he put his black suit on and as he tied his tie, he said, "I will never wear this suit again." I put on my long navy dress and ran a comb through my hair. We were all ready to say goodbye to blessing number one.

Only the family and the eight pallbearers would meet at the funeral home.

They all made their way up to the casket for the last time. Then it was time for Bill and me to go up. No parent should ever have to kiss their child goodbye for the last time. This isn't the way life is supposed to be. I kissed and touched his face for several minutes and then I felt my husband lifting me up.

It was time. They closed the coffin and the boys carried it to the hearse.

The church was full of broken-hearted people. Sharon and I had to be held up as we were escorted to the front pew. I heard the organist playing, "Here I Am Lord". On a good day, that song makes me cry. The pastor read the gospel, "The Prodigal Son" and then he gave his homily. This time he didn't speak of suicide. Instead, he spoke of Billy as if he were a stranger. He was forgetting that Billy made his communion and confirmation with him at that church. He must have forgotten that Billy sat in this very pew every Sunday morning at seven-thirty for fourteen years straight. The pastor also must have forgotten to counsel Billy and pray over him before he left for the Marines.

It was the coldest homily I had ever heard. Later we would find out from many people how disgusted they were with the pastor. My sister-in-law even wrote him a letter.

When he was finished with his sermon, Sharon's best friend got up to read Sharon's eulogy:

My Big Brother Billy......

When we were young I always wanted to be wherever my brother was. When Billy went over to a friend's house he always had to take me with him. I was always the annoying little sister who was continuously following him. Until he got old enough to realize his little sister's friends were pretty cute. After that, I was always included in everything on the condition that I brought the single hot girls.

Billy truly lived every day to the fullest, according to how much money he had that day. He was continuously asking my parents if he could do mundane jobs for a few extra bucks, and it was always spent before he even had it. If he wasn't saving for his next tattoo, he just wanted to go out with his friends and loved treating them to a drink. More than anything, billy loved having fun.

He absolutely loved to laugh, and once he got started it was simply contagious. Whether he was sitting around with his friends telling 'your momma' jokes, or polack jokes with daddy, torturing mommy with disposable cameras, watching the Three Stooges, or simply making fun of me my nicknames included

"Filthy," "The Big C," and "Hooked on Phonics." He had nicknames for everyone. He always loved roughhousing, he would pile drive me, body slam, biff, or gleek on me to drive me crazy, but I could never get mad because it was always for fun. He loved to have fun. When he smiled his soul shined. He had such a tough exterior covered in tattoos and piercings, which he was so proud of. To others, he may have appeared scary, but as soon as he smiled it was clear that he had an enormous heart. I love that we still refer to our parents as Mommy and Daddy. Family always came first to Billy, above all else.

Billy was dealt a few bad hands, he just could never break even. He tried so hard to turn his life around so many times, but as soon as things were looking up, it just never seemed to go his way. He could never catch a break.

In the past few months, Billy was so happy. The future finally seemed bright and he was looking forward to so many things. All he could talk about was being in our wedding and Kevin's wedding. I'm positive there is nothing that will keep him from being there. He isn't gone, he is at peace, and he is here with us and will always be our guardian angel. I'll always love you, Billy.

Your lil' sister Sharon

Thank God for her eulogy. This was the compassion and memories we wanted and needed. Everyone was able to relate to something she said. The mass was over and we followed the casket to the car. We were having Billy cremated so that was the last time we would be seeing the coffin.

Everyone was meeting at a local restaurant for a buffet lunch. As soon as Bill and I returned home we tore our clothes off and threw them out.

Everything!

This was the letter my sister-in-law wrote to our pastor:

Dear Father,

My name is Dolores, you may remember me because I am Bill Costello's sister. I am writing to you because something has been troubling me since my nephew Billy died. I understand that at first, you thought he had taken his own life but when Bill told you that was not true the night before the funeral we thought you believed that it was truly an accident. Billy had no intentions of ending his life. He was drunk and being the guy who was always trying to make his friends laugh just did something so daring and not thinking that anything could hurt him, jumped out of a moving car.

Your homily on the day of his funeral only spoke of sinners and God's mercy. You never once mentioned that you knew Billy as a young beautiful boy who, even though he had times of trouble had so much love in his heart. How he would go out of his way to help people he loved and even people he didn't know. If he saw someone needing help, he never hesitated. His family and friends were very important to him. You never mentioned how he would always watch over is younger sister, Sharon.

I found your homily to be very cold as if you were talking about some criminal in need of mercy, someone you never knew.

I felt you were judging him because you thought he took his own life. I apologize if I too am jumping to conclusions but I have been to many funerals and this one did nothing but make me angry. Homilies at funerals give the family peace and hope. I waited for some kind words about Billy but there were none. My reason for writing to you is that I pray you will talk to Bill and Cheryl to tell them I am wrong and give them your assurance that you know the good person Billy was and that you misunderstood their reason for asking for the gospel of The Prodigal Son. Their reason for choosing this gospel was because, for more than a year now, Billy had been doing so well. He had the same job for a long time and he was very happy lately. He was excited about being part of two weddings. His friend's in April and his sister's in May. He was the best friend a person could and a good son.

This is what I thought I would hear at his mass. I hope you understand what I am trying to say to you. My brother Bill and his family need you now as never before. You are not only their priest but their friend and they need closure now. I pray this letter is taken in the right context. It is never meant to disrespect you and If you feel that is the case, please forgive me.

Sincerely, Dolores Munno

THE CELEBRATION OF HIS NEW

LIFE

It was now December thirty-first. There were about six of Billy's closest friends, plus Sharon, her fiancé, Bill, and myself. We were all in the kitchen making a to-do list. Sharon was determined to fulfill her brother's last wish. We were preparing for a pig roast. After calling several delis, Sharon located a baby pig. The boys

prepared and seasoned the pig. It would have to marinate overnight. I made about twenty-five pounds of sausage and peppers. We also had a twenty-four- pound ham. There would be plenty of food.

Some of the boys put up the food tent outside. They also set up all the tables and chairs. The volleyball net and the horse shoe pits were ready for action. We had just gotten Billy's wallet back from the hospital. It still had eighty-five dollars in it. We used that money to buy the keg of beer. That would have been what Billy would have wanted. Everything was prepared for the big feast the next day.

Only a couple of his friends spent the night. We all watched the clock count down and said our tearful goodbyes to 2004. We were all wondering how things could get better. It was the quietest New Year I think any of our guests ever had seen.

Morning came and everyone was very busy doing their own thing. The pig was put on the grill. It would have to cook for several hours.

All the sodas and beer were put on ice. The weather was unbelievable. It was sixty-seven degrees on January 1 in New Jersey. Soon people began to show up. By one o'clock in the afternoon, there were about one hundred people in my backyard. Most of the people were Billy's friends. Some were family.

There still were a lot of tears, but this time they were shed in between good memories. Everyone had a different story about Billy. One was funnier than the next. We found things we could never imagine him doing. He did everything for a laugh. He lived to laugh. Then one of the boys said, "That could have been one of us." He was

referring to jumping out of a car and getting killed. It seems that they all had done that stunt at one time or another. We know that it was just Billy's time to go. And maybe some of his friends would now have a little fear in their lives.

It was a wonderful day. And it would probably be the last time our yard would be full of so many young people. One of Billy's close friends, a girl, confided in me on how to explain Billy's death. She said, "When people ask how or why he did it. Just tell them he and his friends were extremists, and they all live life to the fullest." Every day I hear those words in my head. She was right.

It's been three months since Billy left us.   I still cry every single day, just not all the time. Some days I seem stronger than others, but then a song plays on the radio and again I'm shot for the day. I take less of the pills these days. Sharon bought me a beautiful necklace with Billy's picture and his name on it. I will wear it every day until I die. We had a special urn made of wood. It has Billy's picture carved into it. Bill bought me an amazing curio cabinet, which we made into a shrine for Billy. I have his baby picture and his first shoes on the top shelf. His ashes are on the second shelf. On the third shelf are his wallet, watch, high school ring, and cell phone. On the bottom are all his pictures from birth to the end.

Filling the curio seemed to make everything complete.

Sharon asked Billy's best friend to take his place in her wedding which will be in two months. He was honored. They were as close as brothers without the blood. Several of Billy's friends got tattoos in memory of Billy, including Sharon. She got angel wings with the initials BBC because that was the initials Billy used. It stood for Billy Bob Costello. She sports the tattoo on her lower back. It measures about six inches in both directions. Bill is going to get a portrait tattoo of Billy on his shoulder.

I prayed to God every night to help me through this, I begged for a sign or something to tell me what it was I was supposed to do. I was woken up one night by this force that seemed to pull me out of the bed. I then went and took my original book out of storage and began to write. I was doing what Billy had told me a year and a half ago. I was finishing my book. He said, "Life doesn't always have a happy ending, so make sure you write about everything." By writing this book, I feel it is my way for a grieving mother dealing with losing one of God's Little Blessings. I will keep Billy deep in my heart and if I have to shed a tear every single day, so be it.

This is a poem written for us by a good friend of the family.

I think it says it all:

I'm Free

Don't grieve for me, for now, I'm free. I'm following the path God laid for me I took His hand when I heard Him call. I turned my back and left it all.

I could not stay another day.

I Have Been Blessed

To laugh, to love, to work or play. Tasks left undone must stay that way. I found that place at the close of the day. If my parting has left a void.

Then fill it with remembered joy.

A friendship shared, a laugh, a kiss. Ah yes, these things, I too will miss. Be not burdened with times of sorrow. I wish you the sunshine of tomorrow. My life's been full, I savored much.

Good friends, good times. A loved one's touch

Perhaps my time seems all too brief. Don't lengthen it now with undue grief. Lift up your heart and share with me.

God wanted me now, He set me free.

Bart's Poem

HERE I GO AGAIN

I bet you are all saying, "here she goes again adding to her story." Well, I am but I promise this is the end for me, there simply isn't anyone else left to write about.

I have to say it has been a whirlwind of emotions for the past twenty years. There have been happy, sad, and very emotional moments. God has made me a very strong woman, that is what I prayed for; strength and independence and I had to work very hard to get to this moment of my life. I've learned how to depend on my inner strength. Prayer was all I had and through all the aches and pains and heartbreaking times, I remained standing. Although I could not see God, I felt him pushing and pulling me through the hell of this world. I knew there were happy times for me waiting as I crawled through life, if that is what you want to call it... life.

Most of the time I wasn't living, I was merely existing. This was how I got by, it was no one's fault, it was God's plan. I know you can't really change the course of your life; it has been planned for you way before you took your first breath. Sometimes you have to just go with the flow of life, even if that means you are just existing.

Those beautiful thoughts in your mind help you through the evil that walks the earth. I'm not saying my husband was evil, he was God's creation which just so happened to have an evil seed in him. That seed took over his mind and destroyed a wonderful person.

I never thought I would be writing another book. I was hoping to keep my life as low-key as possible. After my son Billy's funeral, we were trying to get our lives to a more normal state. My daughter was to be married in May, only 5 months after her brother's death. This did help take my mind out of its depressive state but there was still much sadness.

In April, Billy's friends were getting married. Billy was supposed to be at the wedding party. This was the couple Billy was with when he died in the accident. They had a wonderful wedding where there was a separate table with Billy's picture and a complete dinner setting, alongside the setting was a plaque with a quote by none other than Tinkerbell, it read, "You know that small place between asleep and awake, where you still remember dreaming? That is where I will always think of you." As thoughtful as the gesture was, it was also heartbreaking.

The couple would remain very close to us, in fact, their children were to call me Memom and Bill, Pop-pop. I babysat them from 2 months of age to 5 years of age when they started kindergarten. I would always refer to them as my surrogate grandchildren and it was not until they were much older that they were even aware Bill and I were not their actual grandparents.

My daughter Sharon got married in May 2005. She had a fabulous wedding in North Carolina. It was in a tobacco barn with fields and fields of beautiful landscape. The weather was gorgeous, and guests came from many states to celebrate with us something good for a change. Many friends of Billy's came from New Jersey. There were a lot of sad moments but we somehow managed through it all.

Bill walked Sharon down the grass to the justice of the peace, he looked so handsome as he sobbed the entire way. Then there was the father-daughter dance and again he sobbed. A little while into the evening Bill had asked me to dance, this was our first dance ever and we were now, at the time, married for 27 years. Then Billy's friends lined up, tapping Bill on the shoulder, and one by one they danced with me. I have to say, there was no way to control the tears, they just flooded out. Not just from me, but all the boys too.

Everything about the wedding was perfect. Sharon wouldn't have it any other way. Sharon became pregnant very soon after the wedding and we were so excited to have our first grandchild, a boy who would be called Coletrane.

Coletrane was born on March 7, 2006. Bill and I made a visit to North Carolina for the birth. Bill was a real proud Grandpop.

Actually, a real proud Pop-Pop would be his second name. I visited another time to North Carolina to see the baby and of course my daughter and her husband. While I was there, I began to have sharp pains in the right side of my head, that is where my shunt is located. I could not lie down without having pain, so I slept sitting up. I did not let my daughter know about the pain, she had enough to worry about with taking care of a little child and when I arrived home, the pain seemed to ease, in fact, it went away.

MORE STUMBLING BLOCKS

About two months had passed since my visit to North Carolina. I was in town cleaning a customer's office when I received a frantic phone call from the owner of the office. The owner said I had to come home immediately, that Bill had an accident with the lawn mower. I was only 3 minutes away and as I was pulling into the driveway, I saw police and an ambulance. Bill was sitting in the grass, holding a towel to his left foot. The funny part about it was, that when our friend found him, he sent his wife into my house to get a towel and ice. She came running out and exclaimed, "they only have white towels!" to which he replied, "bring out the dam towels!"

Bill stepped on the reverse before getting on the mower and wound up taking his left heel off, bone and all. Bill was in the Emergency Room when this short, young doctor walked in and said, "mangled foot, we have to remove it." Bill being the loud person he was, and a little intimidating said, "come here Doogie Houser, you're going to save my foot no matter what it takes!" SO that was that 8 months later and 8 surgeries, he was able to keep his foot though there would always be a lot of pain.

Coletrane was going to be a year old and Sharon wanted him to be baptized, which was strange because she didn't want anything to do with religion. Anyway, we had the baptism here in New Jersey. At the after-party I began having terrible headaches, I was rushed to the hospital in Newark where my doctor revised my shunt, it was 27 years old. When I returned from the hospital, Sharon shaved the rest of my head and we were able to get a real cure photo of Coletrane and I, both bald.

After Bill lost half a foot and wasn't able to walk around the yard or farm, I gave away all of our horses. I had to take care of him. It took about a year before Bill started working on the cars again. After all, Bill had undergone, he had become very clingy, and we both had taken so many blows. Billy dying, Bill's accident losing half his foot, and all my head problems. Bill became very jealous and paranoid and the days were really dragging on.

BACK IN THE HORSE BUSINESS

Sharon's mother-in-law was up visiting in New Jersey. She suggested Bill get back into the horse business. She came in as a partner with us. Bill got the spark back in his eyes. We purchased a yearling at the sale so all of is put our suggestions together for the perfect name and we came up with, I AM BILLY COLETRANE. We also purchased a baby from around the corner, his name was NUKEIAM. We raised both of them until they were ready to race. Both horses became pretty good racehorses but not super. We made our rounds back and forth to the farm and racetrack and I continued my visits to North Carolina. Sharon had two more boys, Cash and Hawke. They were all wonderful grandsons, and they would all visit in the summer so Bill actually only got to see them about once a year.

We purchased this one beautiful mare; her name was ARTISTS FLOWER. Unfortunately, she only raced four times, she won a race and then was injured. WE took her back to the farm and decided to breed her. Her first foal was great but developed a heart condition. The next year, Artists Flower delivered, with my help, another Filly. Bill named her ICOMMANDMYSPIRIT since the mare was bred on Good Friday and didn't deliver the first foal until Good Friday the following year and Bill said, "that's what Jesus said on the cross." ICOMMANDMYSPIRIT was a super horse, our pot of gold, the kind of horse every trainer/owner wishes they had.

We spent every waking moment together. To breakfast, to the farm, back to the auto shop, and repeat and one night a week we went to the racetrack. ICOMMANDMYSPIRIT won 35 races in her lifetime and for all the others she got a check for 2nd, 3rd, 4th & 5th. She was amazing. It was so exciting for both of us. I always thought Bill was going to have a heart attack, he would be so anxious.

During this time, my dad's wife passed away. I was like her daughter since she never had children of her own. Now my dad was 90 years old and I had to give him special time. Bill would go to the farm and I would take care of my dad. This meant that my visits to Sharons had to be put on hold. My dad lived on his own for four more years along with SEXY, a rescue dog we got to keep company.

DADS PASSING & BAD TIMES

I arrived at my dad's early one morning, I called out to him and he answered, "I'm in the living room." So I walked down the hall to the living room only to find my dad still in his clothes from the day before, sitting in his recliner he said, "I can't feel my legs." He was paralyzed. He was taken by ambulance to the hospital. I waited for my husband and we went to meet my dad at the hospital. He had had a stroke and would remain in the hospital for a few days before he was moved to a rehab facility closer to our house where I would visit him two times a day, every day. He wasn't progressing and seemed very depressed, I spoke with Bill and we decided my dad would move in with us.

The next morning, I told my dad as soon as he could walk, he would be moving in with us. All of a sudden there was a sparkle in his bright blue eyes. He then went to therapy and began to exercise. He actually thought in the back of his mind that we were going to put him in a nursing home. Not as long as I had the strength to take care of him.

My dad was only at my house for about a month when we hit a brick wall. I walked into his room to bring him his breakfast as he sat in his recliner and he said, "Cheryl, I can't feel my legs again." I asked him, "Do you want to go to the hospital or do you want to stay here?" He knew I meant, is this his last destination?

He said, "I want to stay here, no more hospitals, please can I stay here with you?" At that moment I became a nurse, aid and housekeeper. I was glad I paid attention to the nurses at the rehab so I was able to change his sheets with him in bed, able to bathe and diaper a grown person. It definitely took me a while to adjust and treat him as my patient, not my dad.

It was then that we put my dad's house on the market. The house my grandfather built making it about 125 years old. We were the only family who ever lived in this house and there was over 100 years' worth of stuff collected. Do you know just how hard it was to sort, sell, and get rid of all that stuff? We did this in about 3 weeks and also sold the house in about 2 weeks. I'd say we were pretty amazing, Bill and me.

My dad was bedridden for 5 months. I managed very well by dividing my time between my husband and my dad, or so I thought. My husband always said I wasn't giving him enough time. We did still go to the farm every day and raced once a week. My dad passed away on February 3, 2016. Thank heavens he was eating and drinking almost to the end so his body still had some meat on it. He looked so peaceful with a smile on his face when I found him at 3 a.m.

Now things started to get rough between Bill and me. He would not let me out of his sight. He was constantly accusing me of fooling around behind his back, it was then Bill bought a gun from an older gentleman friend. The very next day I walked into the bedroom and Bill pointed the loaded gun at me, he had that twisted evil face and he said, "I'm gonna kill you and the bastard you're sleeping with!" Life was so insane for me and I was just not able to understand it.

There was no other person in my life. I was with Bill 24/7 yet I stood there with the gun pointed at me less than 6 feet away. I did not turn or even try to get out of the way. I did not cry or tremble. I simply said, "Go ahead and shoot me, there must be a better life than this. I am done arguing. Just shoot me." There was just silence. Finally, I walked out of the room, that was the turning point, and I said, "You need to get help, something is definitely wrong with you." From that day forward the hate started to grow in me. I told a couple of friends about the gun incident and they were horrified. There seemed to be no way to justify his behavior or repair our relationship. My friends slowed up their visits and too, began to despise Bill. I definitely was on my own. I did not want him

to even touch me but of course, we still had sex otherwise he would accuse me of cheating but there were no more feelings that existed, not any good ones anyway. I did not want to be around him at home or in public. The wall was built and getting taller. I continued my life, taking care of the horses, the house, and the yard. I always made dinner and would always be pleasant, never in a bad mood. Anybody that would come visit saw a happy couple. This went on for years, yes it's called Stockholm Syndrome and I was very good at using it as a coping mechanism.

I never thought about leaving, well... I thought about leaving but I would never attempt it. I knew Bill felt if I was gone, he had nothing left to lose. He was now pretty old, and lost his son, his daughter and grandchildren lived far away and didn't speak to him anyway so if I left he probably would have sought me out and killed me. He would also kill anyone who harbored me, and I could never put anyone else's life in jeopardy. I became very good at hiding my feelings, I should have taken up a career as an actress.

TOTAL CONFUSION

Bill started to forget things. Like where he would put his stuff or forget he had already done something. I could not take the accusations anymore and I started taking valium. I just wanted to go away in my own world. I told Bill he had to go to a head doctor because something was definitely wrong. We made his appointment for testing and he went. The day of the appointment was a long day and the doctor told us they would call with any results. Meanwhile, I went on the roof to seal it. I was blowing it off, I remember I was taking Valium and somehow I walked backward off the roof. I landed on my feet but then my body folded in half, and my face hit my knees. My face and inside my mouth were all broken, making it very hard to scream for Bill. He was working on the fence and finally heard me. I told him to call 911. As I lay there on the ground I told Bill, "If I survive this I'm going to be my own person." I was in the hospital for about 10 days. I had crushed my right ankle, and they fixed it with screws and plates. They fixed my nose but the bones in my cheek and the roof of my mouth had to heal themselves. My back was broken in two different areas that took 2 two surgeries and rods and screws. I was recovering at home when Bill's doctor called and said that the deterioration in Bill's brain was normal for his age and I was so angry because I knew there was something mentally wrong with Bill's head.

Recovery took about 6 months but when it was done, I was as good as new, whatever that really means. We were still racing and nothing changed between Bill and me. My visits to Sharons were few, between my surgeries and Bill's insecurities it was much easier to just stay home. We were also delivering foals at our home so I would sit up all night, watching the mare on camera. When she went down, I ran out. It is one of the best feelings – bringing new life into this world.

It's now Spring 2020. The great China virus attacked the United States. Bill had diabetes, COPD, and heart issues so we folded in and got the Moderna Vaccination. After the first shot, we both got COVID. We went back for the second shot, or should I say the shot from hell. Bill had a stroke – his body paralyzed, no control of his bodily functions, not able to speak. It was a nightmare. It took a couple of days before he was actually moving and acting normal. To top this all off, my daughter sent me a text to my husband's phone because I no longer had one. I texted her asking what was wrong and to please give me a call. Her reply was, "I really don't think you want to hear anything I have to say, you both at least haven't for the past 3 years. I'm not going to talk to you any longer on HIS cell phone and Im never gonna be on your bullshit speakerphone conversations anymore! Are you still even allowed to talk to me?" She continued, "I'll never forgive him for taking my best friend away and this is just the tip of the iceberg of what I would need to get off my chest to move forward. So do you still want to talk to me??"

Ok now, remember she sent this text to Bill's phone. Nothing like putting me in the middle of things. I am not the kind of person who argues, in fact, I get quiet, very quiet. I didn't want to argue with Sharon, and I definitely didn't want to argue with Bill, and to top it all off she was angry with both of us because we supported Donald Trump. I knew things were just going to get together now.

The stroke set Bill back really far. There was no more Auto Repair business, it was impossible for him to remember anything. He couldn't drive anymore because he would get lost, he would even drive right past our house, and he would get his pills all mixed up and the paranoia was getting increasingly worse.

I had to take care of all the horses. Bill would help the best he could.

We had a colt that broke his halter so Bill knew he physically couldn't catch him, and he called a horseman to come and put the halter on. I was in the corner of the stall when Bill's friend grabbed the colt by the broken halter, and at the same time, the colt reared up and fell backward, landing on top of me. He snapped my leg, crushed my left ankle, and broke my back... again. This was during COVID, and I once again had to have surgery, this time on my ankle with plates and screws. I had a rod put in my leg from my knee to my ankle and also some more bars were placed in my back.

This time I was only laid up for about 4 months. It was just too much for Bill to do so I started doing all the horses again by myself. Bill had to walk with a cane now and he would fall quite often. Finally, he said, "Let's send all the horses to the farm. That way they would be taken care of properly." He did not want me to get hurt anymore. Once they were at the farm it was like, out of sight, out of mind. We barely went there to visit them; it was too depressing for Bill. He was crying all the time. Finally, he said, "Let's put them in the sale in November." So that's what we did. That was the last straw, it broke Bill's heart to sell the horses.

Cheryl Costello

FINALLY... ANSWERS

It was now over a year since there were any horses on our farm. It was hard to look out the back door and see all the empty barns. It's also been a year of total confusion for Bill. We saw our general doctor and I explained all the problems we had been experiencing. She definitely felt Bill should see a neurologist but because of all the COI+VID nonsense, we had to wait 5 months.

I had to now walk behind him holding his waist otherwise he would fall backwards. He would shuffle his feet and not even move an inch and the crying was constant.

Finally, after 5 months we went to see the neurologist. Bill goes through several tests and after waiting 2 weeks we meet with the neurologist again, she walks into the room, throws a stack of papers on the exam table, and says, "he has vascular dementia, I am not able to help him, he is way too advanced." This was October 2023. Then she said, "Actually, these reports are from 2016." Bill had seen her partner in the practice then and those reports showed what was the beginning of his dementia in 2016, he could have been prescribed medication for his depression, delusions, and paranoia. Life perhaps would have been a little easier to endure.

In January 2024, I found him sitting on the bed with a loaded gun in his hand. He was now confused, he could hardly walk, he was seeing people in his bedroom, and other delusions. He slept 18 hours a day and insisted on going to the bathroom which we never made it there in time. He would eventually fall and I would have to make him crawl to the bed so I could help him up.

Between January 14th to the 16th Bill never closed his eyes. He was so wired. He fell once and I was able to get him up, he fell twice and I called his friend who picked him up like a rag doll. The third time he fell I gave him a pillow and said, "Rest there a while, I don't have the strength." That night he had me make plates of food for the imaginary people in our bedroom. Thank God Hospice finally came. They put him in a hospital bed and told him his legs didn't work anymore so he would have to use a diaper and stay in bed. That was when the switch went off. From that day forward he forgot how to feed himself and couldn't even roll over in bed. That night he also slept like a baby and so did I.

For a little while things got easier. I didn't have to pick him up, his older sister would visit about once a week and it was very hard for her to watch him deteriorate. I became a nurse and I reminded him that growing up I always wanted to be a vet, not a nurse. The bedroom was always full of imaginary people, mostly old friends who had passed on, his mom, and cops. He would say things like Aunt Ida ruined his family, and he would talk about how he had been on his own since he was 14 because Aunt Ida wouldn't let him live in her house when his mom lived there. He would always call out to his sisters, Mary, Dolores & Roz. Some of the medications would have adverse effects on him. He would be so wired and crazy that he would try to climb over the rails of the hospital bed, he was so strong I could hardly control him.

Bill's good friend Vince, the guy who would help pick him up for me, stopped by to say he was moving to Florida. This broke Bill's heart, he had known Vince for forty years and it broke my heart too, we were really going to miss him and he promised he would come visit every time he came up from Florida.

I was trying everything to keep busy. Whenever Bill was asleep, this could be daytime or nighttime, I was busy. I cleaned the entirety of the two shops out, organized all the tools, and began selling stuff on Craigslist and then my girlfriend set me up on Facebook and I started selling items on Marketplace. I really wanted to sell the entire shop equipment for $10,000 but that didn't work so I sold everything, piece by piece and so far, I am up to $9,200, almost met my goal. After everything was cleaned out of the garage I began to paint. I painted everything. The walls were white and the floor was yellow. It looked so bright and brand new. I also painted, or rather, epoxied my bathtub. It went from pink to white and it all looked awesome. I sanded all the radiators and repainted them silver and those were just a few things I did to keep me busy.

I had heard that gas prices were outrageous. I wouldn't know, I really didn't leave the house and only had to fill the gas tank 3 times in 8 months and that was also when I filled the spare cans for the lawn mower.

Finally, summer had arrived and I would mow whenever Bill was sleeping. I would do the food shopping at 7:30 a.m. Didn't have to shop for much because Bill's appetite was depleting. It was Memorial Day weekend when Vince came up for a visit, when he walked in the room, Bill said, "Look at my pollack friend Vince is up from Florida." That was such a shock because at this point Bill didn't even remember who I was. He would always think I was one of his sisters. Also, around this time a good friend stopped by to see Bill, and again, he recognized him with no problem. Bill said., "All you gotta know Jackie Mo!" he had not seen this friend in over 10 years.

Two days later I woke up to the sound of Bill choking. I went over to his bed to find him covered in black vomit. I took pictures for hospice and proceeded to clean him up. It was then I noticed he wasn't speaking and had a vacant stare. Hospice came and I showed them the pictures, the hospice nurse said the term they use for this is coffee grinds. Somewhere in his body is an infection that his body is rejecting. Vince stopped by and couldn't believe how bad he had become in just 2 days. This was the day of the Memorial Day parade so I stopped my niece outside and gave her the update that her uncle was now on oxygen and death was getting close. She connected with the rest of the family at the parade. Later that day his whole family filed through the room to visit, or should I say they came to say their last farewells. Bill said with a smile, "Wow, I have a big family!" This broke my heart because I knew they would never visit again. His sister Mary would continue to come once a week, and his sister Roz and her children would come two times a week.

Bill did have other friends that visited like Ken, Jeanne, and Dante all the way from Argentina. Soon after the coffee grinds incident Bill stopped eating. Occasionally a yogurt or something pureed. He did start talking a little more and would say some really cute things. He would joke with the aide whom he really loved. She would ask who threw the pillow on the floor and he would point to his own baby picture and say, "he did it," or he would make a noise and then say, "I didn't fart."

It was at this time his limbs became stiff, actually more like frozen in place. He was bent like a pretzel and could not be moved without great pain.

NEARING THE END & LAST

WORDS

It was now the late part of June and the nurse was doing a cognitive assessment. She was asking Bill all types of questions:

Nurse: Who is the president? Bill: I don't know.

Nurse: Is it Trump? Bill: No

Nurse: Is it Biden? Bill: No

Bill: Some other Asshole! Nurse: What's your dog's name?

Bill: Sharon (Bill can't hear well)

I told the nurse that he hadn't heard her, he thought she said what is your daughter's name. Mind you, the nurses kept bugging me about getting in touch with Sharon and I always said that Bill did not want that. The nurse then asked Bill, "Do you want to talk to Sharon?" and Bill replied, "Yes." This instantly gave me the guilt that maybe I was keeping her from him. The nurse asked, "What would you say to her if we called her?" and Bill exclaimed loudly, "FUCK YOU BITCH!" It brought about a sense of relief, at least now I knew I wasn't keeping her from him. The nurse then informed me his blood pressure was high. Oh really, I thought to myself, what did she expect?

Bill's mind was in another world. Blank stares into the ceiling, at times there would be one-way conversations, and many times I would have to pretend I saw the people he was talking to and partake in the conversation. Many times I had to tell the ladies to turn when I changed him, his body had lost all its muscle, fat, and ability to move. His pain was extreme and I thank God Bill wasn't aware of the condition he was in. Bill didn't realize he couldn't move or now weighed 75 lbs. I sent a picture to my friend, and she gasped and said he looked like, or even worse than, a holocaust victim.

I had to only have cartoons on the television. The shows that we used to watch were programs like FBI Files, CSI, Buried in the Backyard, etc. If he were to have seen them now he would actually think he was in those situations. He would tell me to watch out because there were dead people on the floor or that he used the backhoe to bury someone in the backyard and many times I would have to shut all the lights out because the police were coming.

It had been about 5 weeks now that Bill had eaten anything. The nurses were baffled as to how a body could survive that long without food. They kept telling me it was because I was giving Bill such good care and this would upset me because I felt like I was prolonging his existence, and not in a good way.

The nurses were convinced there was something going on in his mind that was keeping him here.

Again, I asked Bill if he wanted to speak to Sharon. He said he wanted to make peace with her. He did not want any more anger or arguing so I called my daughter's best friend, well former best friend as Sharon had stopped speaking to her at the same time she stopped talking to her father and I. Her girlfriend calls her up, gets the answering machine, and leaves a message. Two minutes later the phone rings, the friend does not even get the chance to say hello and the first words out of Sharon's mouth are, "Who died?" Her friend proceeded to say, "No one, your dad is very bad and wants to make peace." That was all she got to say. Sharon proceeded to rant and rave about everything and anything. She said she had her own family problems, and her son was sick.

She said she already made peace with her father, (whatever that meant) and she also stated firmly that she was not coming before or after he died and hung up the phone. Her friend sat, sobbing her eyes out, and said, "What are we going to tell Bill?" and I said, "Don't worry, I've got this!" I went over to Bill's bedside and told him a twisted version of the truth. I said, "We just spoke to Sharon and everything is about the same." Coletrane was in the hospital and wouldn't be able to make it here and she conveyed that she already made peace with you therefore now there will be no more arguing. Bill said, "Thank you, that's all I needed to hear."

It was now about the beginning of July. I've been saying prayers with Bill for 8 months and it would take about half an hour each day. I really had the need to ask God to forgive and bless Bill. One day when I was finished, Bill said "I have to talk to God." I said "Okay," and Bill just continued to stare at me then I said, "Oh, you want me to leave?" Bill said "Yes," and I left. About 10 minutes later I returned and asked, "Did you talk to God?" Bill replied, "Yes" and I asked, "What did he say?" and Bill said, "God said I was stubborn!!" Go figure, I could have told him that he was stubborn.

One night I was changing for bed and Bill said to me, "You have to go to the doctor." I asked him, "Why is that?" and he said, "You lost your boobs." As we all know, when you lose weight, the first thing to go is your boobs and I had lost about 25 lbs. throughout this ordeal, so we were at about a total of 100 lbs lost combined. Bill was not in there anymore. Every so often he would seem to visit only for a short time. In these moments he would know me as Cheryl but a lot of the time he called me mom, Mary, or Dolores, his sisters. For a long time, I was everyone but Cheryl. I would just answer in the middle of the night to whomever he called me. He would tell people when they visited that I was the worst warden he ever had. I was apparently more mean and much stricter than the ones he had in jail but in the last two months, he remembered me. Every time I walked into the room he would tell me he loved me. He would tell everyone that I was the best nurse ever and I took the best care of him. I would tell him he could leave and go with Jesus. He would say he was ready and then he would tell me he didn't want to leave me yet. I would explain that I would take care of myself. I have been doing that for the past 2 years. I told him that he had taught me everything I knew, and he would agree with me and say that I was amazing then all of a sudden, he would say that we needed to talk very low because all the people in the room were listening.

The person in that bed was not the evil Bill I knew. He was patient with me, he was caring and sweet. He never got angry with me again. He no longer questioned my doings, he accepted everything I did. Oh my God, this was once again, the man I married. Yes, taking care of him was exhausting and very draining but it was also so rewarding to me. I was able to show love and compassion again. This was not physical love, this was the love shared between two souls. Then one morning Bill said to me, "Do you see the light across the street?" It was daytime so I couldn't see any light but again commented on it and how bright it was. I told him he could go to it and he asked me how since he couldn't walk. I tried to tell him he could just think of the light and float to it but he said he would wait. Through all this, I realized I had to forgive Bill completely in order to give him the care he needed. Every day I prayed to God to give me the strength, compassion, patience, and most of all the forgiveness I needed to take care of Bill, and day by day, the anger lightened, the hatred left and the bad memories disappeared.

I was now there, taking care of the man I truly loved, just as I loved him when we first met. His life was in my hands and I protected him. I wouldn't let the nurses or aides hurt him by moving him unnecessarily and I stayed every minute with him to keep him from undue pain. When we prayed every day we started with Our Father, a Hail Mary, a Novena to St. Jude, a Novena to St. Anne, and a Novena to baby Jesus. Sometimes Bill would say a few verses with me. One day he asked if he could hold Jesus' hand. I always had the statue of young Jesus on the bed while we prayed so as he held the hand of Jesus, I was able to get the most wonderful picture of it. Today it remains framed and on my dresser.

It was the middle of July when the news reported that Donald Trump was shot. I went into the bedroom where poor Bill lay twisted like a pretzel, only his left arm had movement from the elbow down. I proceeded to tell him that someone tried to kill Trump but only got his ear with the bullet. Bill raised his left hand up and hit the bed with it, tears in his eyes. He was loyal to the very end. Another time, also in July, the Aide Bill truly adored was washing his back. He was slightly on his side just looking at me and all of a sudden he says, "She's checking out my ASS!" and the aide nearly fell to the floor. He really hadn't spoken in about a week but out of nowhere, he was able to make us laugh uncontrollably. Then about 2 days passed with no words spoken at all. My niece Cissy was now staying over because we knew it was really close to the end. Cissy was sitting and talking to her Uncle Billy, she would always tell him not to worry about me as she promised to take care of me, and this time Bill started to whisper to her. He asked her to take care of Aunt Cheryl. Cissy promised and came out of the room crying, knowing that this time when he asked, he was saying goodbye.

HIS LAST MOMENTS

Bill has not eaten anything for almost 6 weeks now, he was getting morphine every 2 hours and lorazepam every 4 hours for the past 3 weeks. Thank God they put a catheter in so we no longer had to subject him to the pain that he felt when we would have to change him since his body was frozen in a contorted pretzel position. Then he refused to drink for about 9 days.

Everything took a lot longer than any book had said. He was so stubborn, his poor body now had so many bedsores from not moving.

My niece Cissy was now staying with me to help me through the nights with Bill's breathing which had become very erratic. He would breathe heavily and rapidly for one minute and then forty-five seconds of nothing. This went on for 24 hours straight. His feet and hands were ice cold despite the fact that we was running a fever. I called Lola, she was his original nurse but had left the agency one week prior since she was relocating. I explained his breathing and everything to her and she said she would come right over. She was sorry she was moving and wouldn't be able to be here for the funeral. I gave Bill his morphine at 4:00 pm, Lola went into the bedroom at 4:30 pm to visit with Bill, she was sitting next to the bed talking to him, "Hi Poppy, it's me, Lola, I really miss you but it's time for you to go.

Jesus is waiting." At 4:55 pm I just went in to check on him and I thought he was in the no breathing mode. I was petting his head and Lola came in to check his vitals, with a stethoscope she listened to his breathing and then said, "Mommy, he's gone!" I simply said,

"WHAT?" As much as you're waiting and expecting, it still hits hard.

Every day for 8 months, our dog Jack would lay in my bed watching Bill in his hospital bed. He was afraid to jump on Bill's bed because of the railings so I would pick him up and place him by Bill every day and he would lick Bill's face until Bill couldn't breathe and then I would put him back on my beg and he would watch over Bill vigilantly. Even when I would go outside, he would follow me and then go right back inside to stand guard. On the last 2 days of Bill's life, Jack would go into the office and sit in Bill's recliner, it was as if he couldn't bear it any longer to see his dad like that.

I believe all of this went on for so long because God wanted to make me strong enough to take care of myself. But most of all God wanted me to see Bill through different eyes. You see I had to completely forgive Bill in order to take care of him the proper way. I fell in love with him for the 3rd time even being a vegetable in bed I saw the man I married. He was suffering so much, my heart cried out for him, nobody knew him the way I did and I never gave up on him.

Getting all the pictures together was a very traumatic experience. So, there are so many pictures. He was always so happy and smiling. Many with the whole family, so many of him and I was always so happy. I never really thought of Bill as a handsome man, I saw him as rugged. Rugged like Charles Bronson, Beretta, or Columbo. This is what I fell in love with, a rugged and very confident man. He was so confident in himself that he felt as though he could do anything, and you know what, he really could. So, for the first time now I am looking at all these pictures and I am seeing a really handsome man. I didn't see the man I had grown afraid of, just a very handsome man that I married. I was able to get Father Vona to do the service. He was Bill's favorite priest and so he came out of retirement just to speak for Bill, what a blessing.

Bill's cousin Johnny gave a beautiful eulogy and included my poem in it. Everything was just perfect for Bill.

I had ordered the most beautiful casket covered with all different kinds of flowers, all in various shades of purple.

FINAL PREPARATIONS

I feel purple is a royal color in heaven, not a fact, just my opinion. The funeral home was so accommodating. They displayed our five-foot sign which said I COMMANDMYSPIRIT, Bill's favorite horse. I had a large horseshoe floral arrangement at the service and the card read, "To Bill from all his four-legged kids." There was also a framed picture of the t-shirt Bill was wearing under his funeral shirt and jacket. It's no secret that Bill was such an avid Trump fan and the t-shirt he wore said, "Fuck Biden and Harris!" I just had to make sure Bill was comfortable in his favorite t-shirt for the occasion.

The re-pass was at the Park Nine Diner. Before Bill had gotten ill we had gone to that diner for breakfast every morning for 10 years. They were our surrogate family since we really didn't have any and until this day they still hold a special seat for me.

I would complain to my mom when she was alive, that was 23 years ago. I would say that life would be so much easier without Bill and she would tell me that no matter how much I thought I hated him, I would really miss him if he were gone. No matter how many times I would run those words through my head, I just couldn't understand what she meant.

It is now 2.5 months since Bill passed and still each day, I cry. It's different from when I lost little Billy. It's a totally different feeling. When Billy passed it felt like a piece of my heart was ripped out but when Bill died, it was like all of me was gone and there seemed to be nothing left. All I can hear are my mother's words, "You're going to miss him when he's gone." 23 years later, I now know those words were true and I just wish I had those big strong arms to wrap around me. Loneliness has proven to be pure hell. We did not have much communication for the last 2 years. I knew what he needed, and things just went pretty smoothly. He would tell me every day, several times a day that he loved me. He just had old-time views about things. When it got to where he could no longer speak, he would mouth, "I Love You."

Shortly after Bill's passing, he visited me in a dream. In the dream, I was in bed with our dog Jack, and my new dog Sophie. I was just there petting them both. Bill walked over, looking very healthy, standing straight and tall. As he was walking towards me he asked, "What are you doing?" and I replied, "Cuddling the puppies." It was just then Sophie sneezed and woke me up. I was pissed at her but extremely happy to have seen Bill so healthy, walking and talking. By the way, that was Bill's favorite line to me, "What are you doing?" Anyway, I wrote the dream down and stuck it on the fridge so every time I am in the kitchen I read it as if Bill is always asking me what I'm doing, and as silly as it seems I always tell him what I'm doing at that moment.

Every night for about 4 months I would play a song on Facebook and feature a picture of Bill. I have so many pictures and so many memories. I still remember when I saw him in the coffin for the first time, my breath was taken away. I told him how sorry I was that it ended up this way. If he wasn't bipolar and if he didn't get this awful brain disease, we would have had a much happier marriage. I was so angry at his illness!

It's been exactly 6 months since Bill passed and I can say that some things are a little easier to accept but I still miss his tight hugs. I miss hearing him call out, "sweet pea", "hon" and "Love" among the few. Certain songs come on the radio and I would remember how he would sing them to me, songs like Pretty Woman and I Cross My Heart. He had a beautiful voice and sang straight from his heart.

I believe these feelings are going to be with me forever, I know this because whenever I hear, Until the Twelfth of Never and You Are My Sunshine, I break down crying for my son Billy and it's now been 20 years since he passed. I guess these feelings that will be with me forever are kind of a good thing because I know, that no matter how much time passes, they will always be with me in my heart.

Bill's eulogy written and recited by his cousin John Costello.

William Robert Costello July 22, 1940 - August 7, 2024

I would like to begin by thanking Cheryl for allowing me the honor to speak about Bill. I know words can't take away the pain. That's your feeling. But know what I say today comes from my heart and the deep Love I have for Bill and our family.

For anyone who doesn't know me. I'm Bill's cousin John Costello.

Even at the age of 5 I always loved when Bill would come to visit. His smile and the attention I would receive made me feel so good and special. To me, he was the coolest family member I had ever met. He was an extremely handsome guy with a golden tan, long dark hair, long sideburns, the coolest mustache, and tattoos. It was like having Elvis as a family member. I remember a Christmas time visit and he brings in this large package. After he helped me set it up, I started playing with it. I heard someone saying, "Are you crazy for giving a 5-year-old this gift?" At the time I didn't see an issue. What's wrong with giving a 5-year-old a life-size Plastic Machine gun that shoots? To this day I can't ever remember what happened to that toy.

As years passed on. I got to work with Bill doing Auto Body work. Teaching me how to work with the tools; sanding, taping, painting, while learning some new words along the way. Working at the house was an added bonus.

Bill and Cheryl have always had a love for animals. At times there were 4 or 5 dogs, cats, birds, and horses. It was like a mini petting zoo. Of course, their love for animals helped them be successful at breeding and racing horses for many years. It seemed that there was nothing they couldn't do. Although every family has difficult times, this could have broken them apart forever. But because of their faith, and love for each other Cheryl and Bill overcame many of them. Losing their son Billy being the hardest. Having Cheryl by Bill's side was certainly a Blessing. A wife who is strong in Love, Faith, and gentleness. She has shown Bill the Love Christ has shown by loving him unconditionally. Bill always played the lottery, hoping to hit the biggest Jackpot!! The thing is how many of you know, Bill really hit the biggest jackpot of his whole life? You see it's so much more than the amount of money. Bill hit the jackpot because he had a devoted wife who loved and cherished him and who would not leave his side! No matter how big the storm was, Bill hit the jackpot because he had devoted family and friends. Bill hit the jackpot because of his sobriety for over 25 years. Most importantly Bill and Cheryl believed in a God that was always with them in the darkest times' to get them through it! In closing, I have a poem that I would like to read.

The Poem

The time has come and we must part And say farewell to our dear hearts.

Should the darkness of the newfound life Be brightened by the truthful light?

And pray that God will steer us straight And deliver us from this fearful hate.

We'll walk the grounds of trust and love

And feel the warmth from Him above.

I know now, that we're at peace

And locked-up feelings will be released.

We have nothing to fear in this new way

We're here forever and ever to stay

I love you all, Cheryl

This is the Circle of Life

Blessing #1

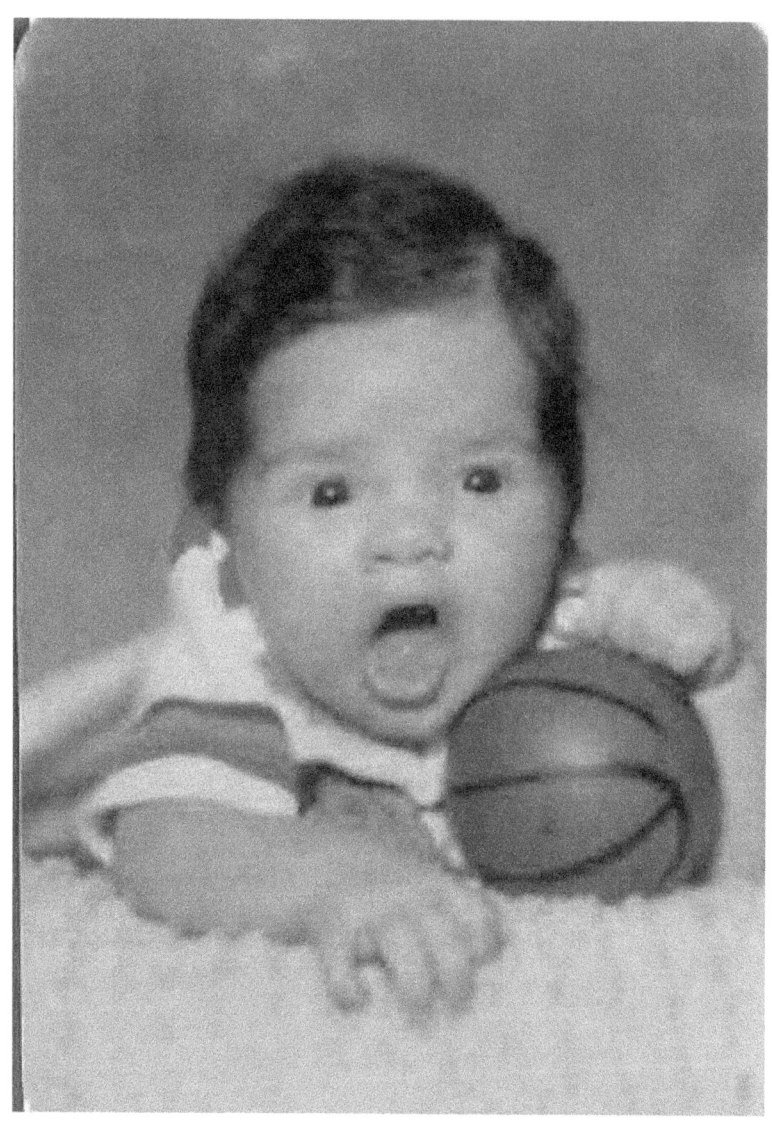

Blessing #1 & #2

Billy & Sharon

Our Big Happy Family

Sharon & Me

Billy the Marine

Billy, 2 Days Before Japan Incident

I'm FREE

Sharon's Wedding

Me & Bill

Bill Talking to Jesus

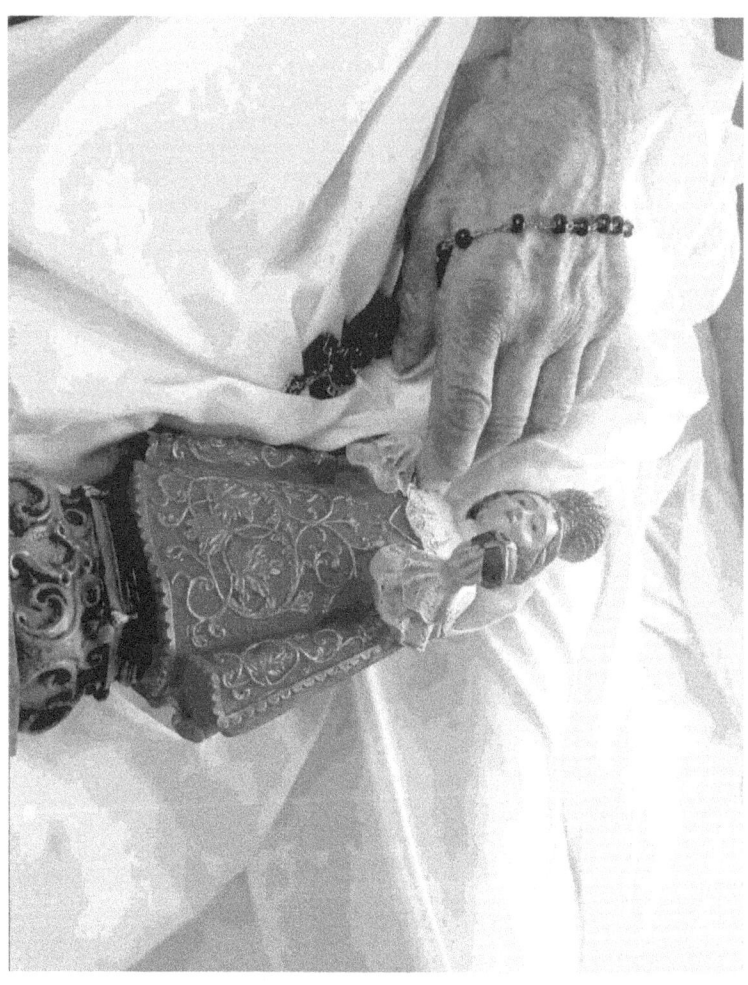

www.ingramcontent.com/pod-product-compliance
Lightning Source LLC
Chambersburg PA
CBHW051144120626
46547CB00012B/939